THE POWER
OF TRANSFORMING
PRAYER

THE POWER

OF TRANSFORMING

PRAYER

 THE CLASSIC WORK BY

J. OSWALD

SANDERS

Discovery House®
from Our Daily Bread Ministries

Requests for permission to quote from this book should be directed to:
Permissions Department, Discovery House,
PO Box 3566, Grand Rapids, MI 49501,
or contact us by email at permissionsdept@dhp.org.

ISBN: 978-1-62707-956-3

Library of Congress Cataloging-in-Publication Data
Names: Sanders, J. Oswald (John Oswald), 1902-1992. author. | Sanders, J.
   Oswald (John Oswald), 1902-1992. Prayer power unlimited.
Title: The power of transforming prayer : the classic work / J. Oswald
   Sanders.
Description: Grand Rapids : Discovery House, 2019. | Previously published:
   Prayer power unlimited. Chicago : Moody Press, 1977. | Includes
   bibliographical references and index. | Summary: "Drawing insights from
   Jesus's teaching on prayer, J. Oswald Sanders offers wisdom from the
   Word to help you develop an effective line of communication with God"—
   Provided by publisher.
Identifiers: LCCN 2019030699 | ISBN 9781627079563 (paperback)
Subjects: LCSH: Prayer--Christianity.
Classification: LCC BV210.2 .S26 2019 | DDC 248.3/2—dc23
LC record available at https://lccn.loc.gov/2019030699

Interior design by Rob Williams, InsideOutCreativeArts.com

Printed in the United States of America
First printing of this edition in 2019

CONTENTS

One Short Hour

Lord, what a change within us one short hour
Spent in Thy presence will prevail to make!
What heavy burdens from our bosoms take,
What parched grounds refresh as with a shower!
We kneel, and all around us seems to lower;
We rise, and all, the distant and the near,
Stands forth in sunny outline, brave and clear.
We kneel, how weak! We rise, how full of power!
Why, therefore, should we do ourselves this wrong,
Or others—that we are not always strong,
That we are ever overborne with care,
That we should ever weak or heartless be,
Anxious or troubled, when with us is prayer,
And joy and strength and courage are with Thee?
                                    —Richard Chenevix Trench
                                              (1807–1886)

Preface

The supreme importance of prayer is tacitly admitted by most evangelical Christians. It is accepted as an article of faith. And yet there are few areas of the Christian life in which there are more regretful confessions of failure and disappointment.

I do not pose as an authority on the subject, only as a fellow student in the school of prayer. I am very conscious of the heights yet to be scaled.

These chapters are the outcome of a series of studies on prayer delivered to a local congregation. The acceptance with which they met has encouraged their reproduction in this form. This is not a book to be read through at a sitting. Its maximum value will be gained if the lessons are studied one at a time and put into practice in daily prayer. It could prove useful for home Bible study groups.

Prayers relating to the theme under consideration, from people of God in all ages, are quoted at the close of each chapter as an indication of how others have approached God. Discussion questions are also appended to each chapter.

A School of Prayer

"Lord, teach us to pray."

—Luke 11:1

Do you long for a more satisfying prayer life? Are your prayers being answered? Are your prayers making an impact on the kingdom of darkness? If not, this book aims to throw a little light on some causes of failure and to suggest scriptural ways in which prayer can become more effective and satisfying—and more to God's glory.

Jesus had drawn His disciples apart for a quiet retreat, a rest from their arduous ministry. He took advantage of the seclusion to pray. His men were around Him. Whether He prayed audibly or not, we are not told. Perhaps they were privileged to listen, but in any case they watched Him at prayer. They saw His face rapt in devotion. They sensed the presence of God and were awed by it.

When He ceased praying, one of the disciples (was it Peter?), doubtless voicing the desire of them all, said "Lord, teach us to pray, just as John taught his disciples" (Luke 11:1). They had seen His mighty miracles, but they did not ask for that power. They had heard His matchless preaching, but they did not ask Him to teach them how to preach. It was His prayer life, His communion with His Father, that they longed to know. He responded at once to their request and proceeded to teach them to pray.

Is this not our paramount need too? Are we not conscious of the untapped possibilities of prayer? If Jesus responded so promptly to the plea of His apostles, will He be less willing to respond to our sincere desire, "Lord, teach us to pray?"

Are you willing to place yourself under His tuition? Will you enter what the saintly Andrew Murray called the "School of Prayer"? Are you prepared to master the lessons on prayer and work them out in practice? If you are willing, you can count on the utmost cooperation of the Holy Spirit, who is the "spirit of grace and supplication" (Zechariah 12:10).

The following chapters are based mainly on our Lord's teaching on prayer, although they are supplemented from other parts of Scripture. They may be regarded as separate lessons to be studied and then carried over into the daily life of prayer. We learn to pray only by praying, however well we may have mastered its theory.

Lord, teach us to pray.

One

Worship and Adoration

KEY TOPIC
How Worship Is Stimulated

Worship the LORD in the splendor of his holiness.

—1 Chronicles 16:29

In a sense, prayer cannot be analyzed, since it is a unity and is the outpouring of the life of the one who prays. Yet in another sense, it can be divided into its constituent elements. "The fact that [prayer] is worship, and the further fact that worship may be expressed in various forms," wrote H. W. Frost, "makes analysis possible.... Prayer is indeed one. But also it is multiform."[1]

There are at least five elements that should be present in a well-balanced prayer life. They are: worship, or adoration; thanksgiving; confession; petition; and intercession. When I first read about the importance of each of these elements, a new world of prayer was opened up. Hitherto my prayers had been almost entirely petition; now my prayer life embraces whole new areas of spiritual experience.

Our Lord's immediate answer to the request of His disciples, "Lord, teach us to pray," was, "When you pray, say: 'Father'" (Luke 11:2). In other words, prayer begins with God. The pattern prayer He gave them was halfway completed before He prayed for personal needs. The concerns and interests of God came first.

This is a supremely important lesson. If God is not given the chief place in our praying, our prayers will be anemic. When our thoughts begin with Him, love is kindled and faith stimulated. So our first lesson will be concerned with Him. We shall consider worship, or adoration, for this is involved in the petition "hallowed be your name" (v. 2).

Dr. R. A. Torrey, who was God's instrument to bring revival to many parts of the world, testified that an utter transformation came into his experience when he learned not only to pray and return thanks, but to worship—asking nothing from God, seeking nothing from Him, simply being occupied with Him and satisfied with Him.

The idea of worship is common to the whole human race. But as generally used, the word *worship* seldom conveys its full scriptural content, which includes the meaning "to bow down or prostrate oneself." Worship is the adoring contemplation of God as He has revealed Himself in Christ and in the Scriptures. It is the act of paying honor and reverence to God. When we pray "hallowed be your name," we are worshiping Him.

F. W. Faber caught the sense of the word in these lines:

How wonderful, how beautiful, the sight of Thee
  must be,
Thine endless wisdom, boundless power, and awful
  purity.
O how I fear Thee, living God, with deepest, tender-
  est fears,
And worship Thee with trembling hope, and peni-
  tential tears.

The Old English form of the word, *worthship*, gives us an interesting insight into its meaning as it implies worthiness on the part of the one who receives the honor. This implication is reflected in the apocalyptic ascription of praise to Christ: "Worthy is the Lamb, who was slain, to receive . . . honor and glory and praise!" (Revelation 5:12).

Worship flows from love, and where there is little love there will be little worship. But even in our love there can be an element of selfishness. We can and should worship God in gratitude for what He has done for us, but our worship reaches a higher level when we adore Him simply for what He is, for the perfection and excellence of His own being.

"I have known men," said Thomas Goodwin, "who came to God for nothing else but just to come to Him, they so loved Him. They scorned to soil Him and themselves with any other errand than just purely to be alone with Him in His presence."[2] Worship, then, is the loving ascription of praise to God for what He is, both in Himself and in His ways.

It is the bowing of the innermost spirit in deep humility and reverence before Him.

When Scipio Africanus returned to Rome after a resounding victory, he rode in triumph, followed by his captives. As he went, he scattered the largess of the victor to the crowds that lined the way. Some were stirred to grateful praise by his gifts; some praised him because he had rolled away from their homes the fear of the invading army; still others, forgetful of their personal benefits, praised his personal qualities—his courage, resourcefulness, liberality. It was in this last group that the highest element of worship was present.

Worship can be wordless. "My soul, wait in silence for God," said the psalmist (Psalm 62:5 NASB). There are times when words are an intrusion, times when the worshiper is hushed in awe of the ineffable Presence and can only be silent to God. A single word can also enshrine a wealth of worship, as when the word *Rabboni* fell from Mary's lips (John 20:16).

But all worship must be "in truth" (John 4:24), that is, free from mere profession or pretense. Brother Lawrence, that saint of the kitchen, learned that to worship God in truth is to acknowledge Him to be what He is and to acknowledge ourselves to be what we are.

How Worship Is Stimulated

A scholar in the school of prayer may feel that God seems far away and unreal, so that attempts to worship Him seem a farce. The question arises, *How can I know God better so that I can worship Him more worthily?*

God has granted a partial revelation of Himself in the wonders of nature. "The heavens declare the glory of God" (Psalm 19:1). We learn there of His almighty power, His transcendent beauty, His unsearchable wisdom. But nature does not reveal Him as a God of love and mercy. Only "in the face of Christ" will we see the full blaze of the divine glory (2 Corinthians 4:6). All the fullness of God dwells in Him in bodily form (Colossians 1:19), and no worship that ignores Christ is acceptable to God, for it is through Christ alone that we have access to the Father.

In Thee, most perfectly expressed,
The Father's glories shine,
Of the full deity possessed,
Eternally Divine!
Worthy, O Lamb of God, art Thou,
That ev'ry knee to Thee should bow.

—*Josiah Condor*

This raises a second question: How can I know Christ, who alone reveals God? The answer is, of course, that we know Christ primarily through the Scriptures, which are the only tangible means of knowing Him. "You study the Scriptures diligently . . . that testify about me" (John 5:39). In them is to be found the complete and satisfying interpretation of God in Christ.

The Scriptures are rich in material to feed and stimulate worship and adoration—especially the Psalms, which is God's inspired prayer book. As you read them, turn them into personal prayer. Vast tracts of truth await our exploration. Great themes abound—God's holiness, sovereignty, truth, wisdom, faithfulness, patience, love, mercy—all of which will call forth our worship.

The use of a good hymnbook in private devotions can also be a great aid to worship. Not all of us find it easy to express our deepest feelings or to utter the love of our hearts to God. We are very conscious of the poverty of our thoughts of God and the inadequacy of the words in which we express them. But we can appropriate the outpouring of worship and praise of men and women whom the Spirit has gifted to express these thoughts in verse. Try using a hymnbook regularly.

We should guard against the idea that worship is confined to the realm of thought, for Scripture links worship with service. During the temptation in the wilderness, our Lord quoted the Old Testament: "*Worship* the Lord your God, and serve him only" (Matthew 4:10, italics added; compare Deuteronomy 6:13). We should not separate what God has joined. Worship is no substitute for service, nor is service a substitute for worship. True worship will inevitably find expression in loving, sacrificial service.

PRAYER

Worthy of praise from every mouth,
    of confession from every tongue,
    of worship from every creature
Is Thy glorious Name, O Father, Son and Holy Ghost;
    who didst create the world in Thy grace
    and by Thy compassion didst save the world.
To Thy majesty, O God, ten thousand times ten thousand
    bow down and adore,
Singing and praising without ceasing, and saying,
    Holy, holy, holy, Lord God of hosts;
Heaven and earth are full of Thy praises;
    Hosanna in the highest.

—Nestorian Liturgy

QUESTIONS

1. What does it mean to "worship in the Spirit and in truth" (John 4:24)?

2. Bishop Moule said, "Worship will be a powerful, secret means to our spiritual growth." In what ways will worship stimulate such growth?

Two

Thanksgiving

KEY TOPIC
Thankful for Everything?

Give thanks to the LORD.

—Psalm 118:1

The second crucial element in prayer is thanksgiving, which is the glad and appreciative acknowledgment of the benefits and blessings God gives either to us or to others. It is an integral part of prayer, not an addendum to it.

Thanksgiving is to be distinguished from worship, for thanksgiving is not so much occupation with the perfection of God as it is the grateful acknowledgment of the love and kindness He has lavished on us. Worship easily and naturally leads us to thanksgiving, for God's perfection finds expression in the daily gifts and blessings He gives.

Even if Scripture did not exhort us to give thanks always and for all things, common courtesy would accord a prominent place to thanksgiving in our prayer lives, for we are constantly at the receiving end of God's generosity. Appreciation is the basis of healthy human relationships, and it is surely no less important in our relationship with God. Aristotle called Memory the scribe of the soul, and it is good for us to let her do her work as she calls to our minds all of God's help and blessing in the past.

The Psalms abound in thanksgiving. "Praise the LORD, my soul, and forget not all his benefits" (Psalm 103:2). "Give thanks to the LORD, for he is good; his love endures forever" (Psalm 118:1).

The prayers of our Lord were not lacking in this element. The occasions on which it is recorded that He gave thanks are significant but rather unexpected: At the grave of Lazarus (John 11:41); when He fed the five thousand (John 6:11); when the seventy returned with shouts of victory (Luke 10:21 KJV); when He instituted the Lord's Supper, giving thanks for the bitter cup He was to drink (Luke 22:17, 19).

We too should call to mind the Lord's dealings with us— His mercies, which are new every morning (Lamentations 3:22–23), and the temporal gifts that recur with such regularity. We are unconscious of a great many of our blessings; they therefore go unacknowledged. "I have experienced today the most exquisite pleasure that I have ever had in my life," said a young invalid. "I was able to breathe freely for about five minutes."

Psalm 103 is a classic of worship blended with thanksgiving. A paraphrase of it by Dr. A. B. Bruce provides a model for our emulation:

God is a beneficent Being. He delights to bestow penitence, He forgives sin, heals diseases, saves life, crowning His worshipers with garlands of love and mercy, and making their hearts young with gladness. He is a righteous God who espouses the cause of the oppressed and shields them from wrong; a magnanimous God, who bears patiently our shortcomings with a Father's heart, full of pity towards frail men subject to infirmity and pain. He is mighty as well as merciful, sitting in majesty on His heavenly throne and ruling as King over all, receiving perfect obedience from the manifold powers of His universe, which do His will and show His glory.[1]

The psalmist's heart overflowed in thanksgiving and praise as he meditated on these themes, but he was conscious of the tendency that we know only too well—failure to give thanks for blessings received and prayers answered. So he apostrophized his soul: "Bless the LORD, O my soul, and *forget none of His benefits*" (Psalm 103:2 NASB, italics added). We should have a definite time every day when we remember the Lord's benefits with gratitude.

THANKFUL FOR EVERYTHING?

Thanksgiving is not difficult when it flows from our recognition of the temporal and spiritual blessings that we consider desirable. But what of the burdens and disciplines, the sufferings and sorrows of life? Surely we cannot be expected to give thanks for those! Yet this is exactly what God does expect us to do. We are left with no option if we are His obedient children. "Give thanks *in all circumstances*" (1 Thessalonians 5:18, italics added). "*Always* giving thanks to God the Father *for everything*" (Ephesians 5:20, italics added). These commands are devastatingly inclusive.

No one would suggest that this is always easy, but it is always possible, or God would not expect it of us. There is an Arab proverb that says, "All sunshine makes a desert," and it is true that if life were all joy and prosperity unmixed with sorrow and adversity, our characters would be immeasurably the poorer. Our loving Father knows the exact proportions in which to mix these ingredients, and we should thankfully and without question accept His dealings with us as the very best for us.

The correct response of the heart is expressed in *The Scottish Prayer Book*: "We praise Thee for the grace by which Thou dost enable us so to bear the ills of the present world, that our souls are enriched by a fuller experience of Thy love, a more child-like dependence on Thy will, and a deeper sympathy with the suffering and the sad."

On his way to exile, Chrysostom exclaimed, "Thank God for everything!" Thanking God in one of his matchless letters, Samuel Rutherford wrote, "O, what I owe to the furnace, the file and the hammer of my Lord Jesus!"

A missionary was greatly discouraged. He knew that his work was not progressing as it should. One day, while visiting another missionary, he saw a motto card on the wall: Try Thanksgiving! It was an arrow to his soul. He realized suddenly that this element had been largely missing from his prayers. There had been plenty of asking God for things he desired and needed; he had asked desperately at times but had forgotten to thank Him for what he received.

So this missionary began to count his blessings and to pour out his heart in thanksgiving. At once the power of the Spirit began to surge through him, and the work at his missionary center began to prosper. His lack of thanksgiving had been quenching the work of the Holy Spirit. Have we been guilty of the same sin?

An old couplet runs, "Prayers and praises go in pairs, they have praises who have prayers," and this should be true of us. John Newton, the converted slave trader, used to give thanksgiving a practical twist by saying that true thanksgiving is thanksliving.

When we reach heaven and are in the immediate presence of God, other aspects of prayer will cease, being no longer necessary or appropriate, but thanksgiving and worship will continue throughout eternity.

PRAYER

Father, with thankful and humble hearts we appear before Thee. We would thank Thee for all the benefits that we have received from Thy goodness. It is to Thy blessing that we owe what success we have found. Every opportunity for doing good, each victory we have gained over ourselves, every thought of Thy presence, are alike Thy gifts to us. The best thanksgiving we can offer Thee is to live according to Thy holy will.

—Michael Sailer

QUESTIONS

1. Is it possible to be genuinely thankful for everything? If so, in what sense?

2. What reflex blessing does thanksgiving bring to our lives?

❧ *Three* ❧

Confession

I will confess my transgressions to the LORD.

—Psalm 32:5

When we recall the all too frequent times we have failed to give God thanks, we realize we have often deserved the rebuke that our Lord directed to the nine ungrateful lepers whom He had healed, but who failed to return to thank Him: "Were not all ten cleansed? Where are the other nine?" (Luke 17:17).

Ingratitude is not an amiable infirmity but a sin. Shakespeare called it, "Ingratitude, thou marble-hearted fiend." "Ungratefulness is theft," said Martin Luther. And we must all plead guilty to the charge in greater or lesser degree. This sin and failure leads us to the theme of our third lesson.

The book of Psalms abounds in thanksgiving, and can be described with equal truth as the world's greatest confessional literature. "Is it surprising," asks A. Jean Courtney, "that the place where God is most praised should be where we read most about penitence? I suggest it is just what we might expect. The more we think of God's gifts, the smaller our own gifts to Him appear. No one suffers from self-righteousness who spends much time in prayer."[1] Confession is the third essential element in prayer.

The Greek word for *confession* means "to say the same thing, to admit or declare oneself guilty of what one is accused of." When I confess my sin to God, I am agreeing with Him in His judgment of its guilt and seriousness. I am viewing my sin from His perspective. We are talking the same language about it, and I am taking sides with Him against it. Note the operative verbs in David's confession recorded in Psalm 32:5: "I acknowledged ... [I] did not cover up.... I will confess."

No confession that is not sincere and explicit will either reach God's ear or quiet an accusing conscience. This is made clear in 1 John 1:9: "If we confess our sins, he is faithful and just and will forgive us our sins and purify us from all unrighteousness." Our confession, to be acceptable, must be not of sin in general but of sins—individual acts of sin.

A general confession is sometimes appropriate, for there are many sins of which we are unconscious or that we have overlooked. This, however, does not dispense with the necessity of a frank and full confession of specific sins. The confession should be made the moment we are conscious of having sinned and should not be delayed until a more convenient time. We have the assurance that the moment we sincerely confess, that moment God freely forgives us and fellowship is restored.

The extent of confession poses a problem to some sensitive and overscrupulous hearts. Is it sufficient to make confession to God alone, or should we confess to others or make public confession? The answer is that there are three kinds of confession that correspond to three kinds of sin.

1. *Secret confession.* When the sin is against God alone, then the confession need be to God alone. To confess to someone else would serve no purpose other than to give that person a knowledge of the sin, and there is no benefit in that.

2. *Private confession.* Some sins are against people as well as against God. The general principle is that the confession should be coextensive with the sin. Whenever possible, we should make confession to the offended party as well as to God. The prodigal's sin was against his father as well as against his God. When he made confession, he confessed rightly: "Father, I have sinned against heaven and against you" (Luke 15:21). Confession to God would have been inadequate and would not have brought peace of conscience, nor would it have restored him to the old filial relationship with his father. Once full confession was made, restoration was complete.

Our Lord gave clear instruction on this point. "Therefore, if you are offering your gift at the altar and there remember that your brother or sister has something against you, leave your gift there in front of the altar. First go and be reconciled to them; then come and offer your gift" (Matthew 5:23–24). The order is: First, go; then be reconciled; then, come to present your gift.

3. *Public confession.* When the sin is public—against some group or church—the confession should be as public as was the sin. In this way the sin can be forgiven, confidence can be restored, and fellowship can be renewed. The very act

of public confession often has a salutary effect that is likely to deter a repetition of the sin.

Some people suggest that even secret sins should be publicly confessed. Scripture does not seem to warrant it. Where this has been done, much harm has sometimes resulted. As someone put it, although God knows all our thoughts and deeds, other people do not share His omniscience, nor need they. It is our social sins that we need to confess publicly, not our secret thoughts and secret acts of sin.

In times of revival, the confession of sins in public has sometimes occurred. But this has been the spontaneous, almost irresistible outpouring of a heart deeply convicted by the Holy Spirit. In these cases, the pressure of the Spirit on the heart is so strong that relief comes only with confession. But spontaneous confession under these circumstances and in the glow of a movement of the Spirit is a different thing from a confession that is not required by Scripture and not pressured by the Holy Spirit. These spontaneous confessions are extraordinary occasions and not the norm.

Contrition, or penitence, will accompany true confession. Contrition is such a deep grief of heart for sin that it becomes resolution to have done with that sin. Professed penitence without the purpose to forsake the sin confessed is insincere and a mockery. Similarly, confession and professed contrition without a resulting change in lifestyle are without meaning and are unacceptable to God.

The depth of contrition of the prodigal son was seen in the confession and request he made to his father: "I am no longer worthy to be called your son; make me like one of your hired servants" (Luke 15:19).

PRAYER

Most gracious, almighty God, full of lovingkindness and longsuffering: we confess to Thee with our whole heart our neglect and forgetfulness of Thy commandments, our wrong doing and speaking and thinking, the hurts we have done to others, and the good we have left undone.

O Lord, blot out the transgressions that are against us for Thy goodness and Thy glory, and for the sake of Thy Son, our Savior, Jesus Christ.

—Anonymous

QUESTIONS

1. Is there a place for sharing the knowledge of some personal sin with a trusted friend and counselor?

2. What is the difference between the cleansing mentioned in 1 John 1:7 and that in 1:9?

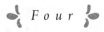

Four

Petition and Intercession

KEY TOPICS
Petitions
Prayers
Intercessions
Practical Application

Petitions, prayers, intercession . . . for all people.

—1 Timothy 2:1 NIV

In our fourth lesson, we turn from the godward aspects of prayer to those with respect to people. These are petition, when we are concerned about our own needs, and intercession, when we are concerned with the needs of others.

There are no fewer than twelve Hebrew words in the Old Testament and five Greek words in the New Testament that are translated "prayer." Our focus is on three of these New Testament words that are used by Paul in 1 Timothy 2:1. "I urge then, first of all, that petitions, prayers, intercession and thanksgiving be made for all people"—petitions, prayers, intercession. Let us examine them more closely.

PETITIONS

This word *petition* is derived from the Greek word meaning "to beg, to lack." It can be and is used of both God and humans. It refers in 1 Timothy to petition for one's personal needs. The picture behind the word is that of a beggar sitting at the side of the road, begging for the help of the king as he passes by. It expresses destitution and inadequacy, inability to meet one's own needs, and total dependence on another. It is need expressed in a cry.

When we come to God with our petitions, we come humbly and expectantly to the throne of grace, deserving nothing, but hoping in God's mercy. We respond to the gracious invitation: "Let us then approach God's throne of grace with confidence, so that we may receive mercy and find grace to help us in our time of need" (Hebrews 4:16).

So *petitions* are pleas for the supply of a definite need keenly felt. Petition always has specific situations in view.

PRAYERS

The English word *prayers* in 1 Timothy 2:1 does not accurately or adequately reflect the meaning of its Greek equivalent. It is a more general term than *petitions* and is used of God alone. The Greek word is a combination of *pros*, "by the side of," and *euchomai*, "to wish." As used here, then, the word *prayers* means prayer-wishes that are expressed in the presence and by the side of another. The other is, of course, our heavenly Father.

One good suggestion concerning the application of *prayers* is that the word refers to needs that are always present, in contrast to *petitions*, which have specific situations in view. For example, we offer *prayer* for the forgiveness only He can impart or for the strength only He can give. The word is very wide in its meaning.

The term *prayers*, then, expresses the Spirit-begotten instinct to turn to God in every hour of need and breathe out our prayer-wishes to Him, just as John's disciples did to Jesus (see Matthew 14:12).

INTERCESSIONS

In petitions and prayers, we are concerned about ourselves and our own needs. In intercession, we are concerned about the needs and interests of others. *Intercession* is the unselfish and altruistic aspect of prayer.

The idea behind the Greek word is "to fall in with a person, to draw near so as to converse freely, and hence to have freedom of access." It is the word used to describe a child who goes to its father in behalf of another or a person who enters a king's presence to submit a petition.

In intercession, the believer is acting as an intermediary between God and other people. We forget ourselves and our own needs in our identification with the needs of the one for whom we pray. The prayers of Abraham for the people of Sodom (Genesis 18:23–33) and of Moses for Israel (Exodus 32:1–14) are classic examples of intercession.

In intercession there are reflex benefits to the one who prays, as well as direct benefits to the one for whom intercession is made. Henry Martyn observed that at times of inward dryness and depression he had often found a delightful revival in the act of praying for others' conversion or sanctification or prosperity in the work of the Lord. His dealings with God for them about these gifts and blessings were for himself a means of grace and blessing.

As we engage in this ministry, the thought of the intercession of our great High Priest is a source of comfort and stimulus. Lilias Trotter of North Africa told how the thought of Christ's intercession took on a new preciousness for her. She was reading of one to whom God had given a wonderful gift of prayer. The thought came to her, *O that we had someone among us who could pray like that!* And then, almost with the vividness of an audible voice, came the further thought, *Is not Jesus enough?*

PRACTICAL APPLICATION

In order that God's glory may be secured and our prayer lives enriched, it is suggested that we review our daily prayers and so arrange them that each element—worship, thanksgiving, confession, petition, and intercession—finds a place. In the morning, perhaps, worship, petition, and intercession will have prominence; in the evening, confession, thanksgiving, and intercession.

PRAYER

We beseech Thee, Lord and Master, to be our help and succour. Save those among us who are in tribulation; have mercy on the lowly; lift up the fallen; show Thyself to the needy; heal the ungodly; convert the wanderers of Thy people; feed the hungry; raise up the weak; comfort the faint-hearted. Let all the people know that Thou art God alone, and Jesus Christ is Thy Son, and we Thy people and the sheep of Thy pasture.

—Clement of Rome

QUESTIONS

1. God knows our needs before we ask Him. Why does He sometimes require us to keep on asking?

2. Does our intercession cause God to change His mind?

Five

The Matchless Teacher

... with strong crying and tears ...

—Hebrews 5:7 KJV

Our most wonderful lesson and our greatest inspiration in the holy art of prayer come from Him who not only spoke as no one ever spoke (John 7:46), but prayed as no one ever prayed. It is Luke who especially captures for us the teaching and habits of prayer in the life of our Lord.

We are inclined to think, are we not, that the human needs of our Lord were less real and pressing than our own and that somehow His human nature was aided and sustained by His divine nature in a way that ours cannot be.

Consequently, it is easy to feel that His need of prayer was surely not so desperate as ours.

But a moment's thought will correct this misconception. Did His deity lessen the intensity of His anguish in the Garden of Gethsemane? Did it banish His hunger or dispel His weariness? The whole testimony of the Gospels leads to the view that His deity in no way affected the reality of His human nature. The only difference is that He did not sin. His prayers were as real and intense as those of any other person.

This truth will be borne out by a study of His prayer life, and let me suggest that you make this a special, personal study. So completely did He renounce the independent exercise of His divine powers and prerogatives that, like the weakest of His followers, He became dependent on His Father for all things. Just as we do, He received His daily and hourly needs through the medium of prayer.

> Why need he pray, who held by filial right,
> O'er all the world alike of thought and sense,
> The fullness of his Sire's omnipotence?
> Why crave in prayer what was his own by might?
> Vain is the question,—Christ was man in need,
> And being man his duty was to pray.
> The son of God confess'd the human need,
> And doubtless ask'd a blessing every day.
> Nor ceases yet for sinful man to plead,
> Nor will, till heaven and earth shall pass away.
>
> —*Hartley Coleridge*

WHERE DID HE PRAY?

He prayed in solitude. If prayer is the Christian's vital breath, the Christian's native air, it was no less so to our Lord. Prayer was the natural atmosphere of His life. Whenever possible, He sought solitude so that He could commune with His Father. It has been remarked that there are three kinds of solitude—the solitude of time, the solitude of place, and the solitude of spirit. Jesus experienced all of these.

Robert E. Speer notes that one of our Lord's two prayers of deepest power was offered before midnight at the temple gates (John 17), the other just after midnight in Gethsemane (Matthew 26:36). He used to spend whole nights in prayer (Luke 6:12) and would rise to pray long before sunrise (Mark 1:35).

He also chose secluded places so that He, sometimes with His disciples, could pray undisturbed. The mountains, the desert, a garden were favorite haunts (Matthew 14:13, 23; Mark 6:46; Luke 5:16; 6:12; John 18:2).

Even in the midst of crowds He experienced a solitude of spirit. Consider the paradoxical clause of Luke 9:18: "Once when Jesus was praying in private and his disciples were with him." He apparently possessed such powers of concentration and abstraction that He did not allow even the presence of His friends to disturb the solitude of His spirit. His longest recorded prayer (John 17) was prayed in the presence of others.

He prayed in different postures. While posture is secondary to attitude of spirit, it is instructive to note that at times Jesus prayed when standing, just where He happened to be at the moment (Matthew 14:19; John 11:41). At another time He knelt (Luke 22:41). On yet another occasion He fell on His face (Matthew 26:39). We might well ask: If the Son of God got down upon His knees and at times fell on His face before God, what attitude should we ordinary mortals assume as we enter the divine presence?

He prayed in secret. Much of His prayer life was concealed even from those closest to Him. His own practice was reflected in His command to His disciples: "But when you pray, go into your room, close the door and pray to your Father, who is unseen"—shut in with God, shut out from all else. He taught them that secret prayer brought open reward. "Then your Father, who sees what is done in secret, will reward you" (Matthew 6:6). Near the close of His ministry, these poignant words occur: "Then they all went home. But Jesus went to the Mount of Olives" (John 7:53–8:1)— probably to spend the night in secret vigil.

> How oft He sought the mountain top, and knelt
> upon its crest,
> To pray, and lay His weary Head upon His Father's
> breast.
> Before He called the Twelve to Him, He prayed all
> night alone,
> And when the day began to dawn, He chose them
> for His own.
>
> —*Great Commission Prayer League*

WHEN DID HE PRAY?

He prayed in the morning, at the gateway of the day (Mark 1:35). *He prayed in the evening,* when the day's work was over (Mark 6:46).

Great crises were preceded by prayer. It was "as he was praying" at His baptism that heaven was opened and the Holy Spirit descended on Him (Luke 3:21–22). This was the watershed of His life and ministry, for He was identifying Himself with the godly remnant of the apostate nation.

He prayed in the hour of His popularity, the time when so many are swept off their feet. When great crowds were thronging Him, "Jesus often withdrew to lonely places and prayed" (Luke 5:16). The glamour of popular approval never carried Him away, for He was fortified by prayer.

He selected the twelve apostles, a seemingly unimportant yet in reality epoch-making event in world history, *only after a night of prayer* (Luke 6:12–13). To them He was to commit the responsibility of carrying His gospel to the ends of the earth.

It was after a special time of prayer that He opened His heart to His disciples and shared with them the dread fact of His approaching suffering and death (Luke 9:18, 21–22).

It was while He was in the act of prayer that the majestic transfiguration scene was enacted, when "the appearance of his face changed, and his clothes became as bright as a flash of lightning" (Luke 9:29), and the approving and authenticating voice of the Father was heard (v. 35). Prayer was the cause, transfiguration was the effect. Is there a lesson here for us?

Great achievements were preceded by prayer. Many of His miracles followed prayer: the feeding of the four thousand (Matthew 15:36); the feeding of the five thousand (John 6:11); walking on the water (Matthew 14:23–33); the raising of Lazarus (John 11:41–42); the healing of the insane boy (Mark 9:14–29). Each of these miracles was linked with the prayer that preceded it, and this is probably true of His other miracles.

Great achievements were followed by prayer. When confronted with great crises or with demanding tasks, we turn instinctively to prayer. But once the crisis is over, the task achieved, we tend to lean again on our own abilities or wisdom. Jesus guarded against this evil by following such occasions with prayer, and we would do well to imitate our divine Exemplar. After what had been perhaps one of His most successful days, instead of courting the popularity of the crowd, He dismissed them and sought solitude for prayer (Matthew 14:23).

Great pressure of work was a call to prayer. Our Lord's life was exceptionally busy. He worked under constant pressure. At times He had no leisure even for meals (Mark 6:31). But whatever the pressure, He made sure that prayer did not become a casualty. To Him busyness was a call to devote extra time to prayer (Mark 1:32–35; Luke 5:15–16; John 6:15).

Great sorrows were faced with prayer. The Man of Sorrows suffered deeply at the hands of His own people. Added to this was the disappointment of His intimate followers' chronic lack of insight and understanding. But the darkest abyss was being forsaken by His Father when Jesus assumed the sins of the whole world. For this He fortified Himself in prayer (Matthew 26:36–46).

He died praying. The hour and suffering of death were powerless to quench the habit of a lifetime. His last utterance was one of trusting prayer: "Father, into your hands I commit my spirit" (Luke 23:46).

HOW DID HE PRAY?

A large field may be seen through a small chink in the fence. While it is true that only a small segment of our Lord's life is preserved for us in the Gospels, what is recorded by inspiration of the Spirit has been carefully selected and may be regarded as representative. His recorded prayers, therefore, afford a rich insight into His heart and provide much material for emulation.

His Father's glory was His consuming passion. He summarized His life's work in seven words: "I have brought you glory on earth" (John 17:4). This was the focus of His prayer life. He secured God's glory by completing the task entrusted to Him.

Thanksgiving was intermingled with worship and petition. Adoring thankfulness constantly welled up in His heart. Whether He was walking in bright sunlight or in dark shadow, He did not forget thanksgiving.

Confession of sin found no place in His devotional life, as it must in ours. This was because there was never any consciousness of defilement or sense of distance from His Father. On the contrary, He asserted, "I always do what pleases him" (John 8:29). No occasion for confession ever arose.

Communion with His Father bulked large in His prayers, whereas petition for personal needs occupied only a minor place. Amid earth's pollution, He pined for the celestial air.

His high-priestly prayer recorded in John 17 is an example of communion with God at its highest.

Intercession also held an important place and included the interests and spiritual advancement of His disciples. His prayer for Peter opens a wonderful line of truth: "Simon, Simon, Satan has asked to sift all of you as wheat. But I have prayed for you, Simon" (Luke 22:31–32). He prayed for His enemies, even for those who crucified Him (Luke 23:34).

His prayers were invariably answered. "I knew that you always hear me" (John 11:42) was His testimony. This assurance rested on the fact that He knew He always prayed in line with the will of God.

From the gospel records it seems clear that of all His excellences of character, it was His prayerfulness that most impressed His apostles. "The Lord Jesus is still praying," wrote S. D. Gordon. "Thirty years of living; three years of serving; one tremendous act of dying; nineteen hundred years of prayer. What an emphasis on prayer!"[1]

PRAYER

Blessed Lord, in lowly adoration I would bow before Thee.
Thy whole redemption work has now passed into prayer:
all that now occupies Thee in maintaining and dispensing
what Thou didst purchase with Thy blood is only prayer.
Thou ever livest to pray. And because we are, and abide in Thee,
direct access to the Father is always open, our lives can be ones
of unceasing prayer, and the answers to our prayers are sure.

—Anonymous

QUESTIONS

1. Write down definite ways in which it is possible for you to follow the example of the Master in prayer.

2. Since Jesus was never out of touch with His Father, why do you think He found prayer so necessary?

Pleading the Promises

... his very great and precious promises ...

—2 Peter 1:4

The original owners of the fabulous Mt. Morgan gold mine in Queensland, Australia, toiled for many years on the mountain's barren surface eking out a frugal living, unaware that beneath their feet lay one of the richest deposits of gold the world has ever known. Their potential wealth was incalculable, but they lived on the breadline because they were ignorant of the wealth they possessed. The same is true of many Christians. In the promises of Scripture we have "boundless riches" (Ephesians 3:8), but because we fail to appropriate them, we live in comparative spiritual poverty.

"Every promise of Scripture is a writing of God," said Charles Haddon Spurgeon, "which may be pleaded before Him with this reasonable request, 'Do as Thou hast said.' The Creator will not cheat the creature who depends upon His truth; and far more, the heavenly Father will not break His word to His own child."[1]

WHAT IS A PROMISE?

A promise is a written or verbal declaration that binds the person who makes it to do or forbear a specified act. When used of God, it is His pledge or undertaking to do or to refrain from doing a certain thing. Such promises form the basis of the prayer of faith. It is through prayer that these promises are turned into the facts and factors of our Christian experience.

The validity and the dependability of a promise rest on the character and resources of the one who makes it, just as the validity of a bank check depends on the integrity and bank balance of the one who signs it. The holy character and faithfulness of God make His promises credible. "He who promised is faithful," testified the writer of the letter to the Hebrews (10:23). "Not one word has failed of all the good promises he gave through his servant Moses," said Solomon to the whole assembly of Israel (1 Kings 8:56).

God's promises are thus bound up with His character and rest on four of His divine attributes: (1) His *truth*, which makes lying impossible; (2) His *omniscience*, which makes His being deceived or mistaken impossible; (3) His *power*, which makes everything possible, and (4) His *unchangeableness*, which precludes vacillation or change.

So when we come to God armed with one of His promises, we can do so with the utmost confidence. We can share Abraham's unstaggering trust. "Yet he did not waver through unbelief regarding the promise of God, but was strengthened in his faith and gave glory to God, being fully persuaded that God had power to do what he had promised" (Romans 4:20–21).

The Range of the Promises

One of the astonishing features of the Bible is the wide range and variety of the promises it contains. Peter calls them "his very great and precious promises" (2 Peter 1:4). A diligent but anonymous Bible student once claimed that there are no fewer than thirty thousand such promises awaiting appropriation. Whether this claim is true or not, it is certain that the larger proportion of these verses relate to prayer.

It is noteworthy that all the universal terms of the English language—*whatever, whenever, wherever, whoever, all, any, every*—are repeatedly used in connection with prayer, as though to encourage our timid faith. In your reading, watch out for these inclusive and expansive words. God's promises thus cover the whole range of human need. There will be no conceivable circumstance of life for which there is not an appropriate promise waiting to be claimed. These promises are keys that will open every lock, for they cover the whole realm of human experience.

There are heights of sweet communion that are
    awaiting me,
There are ocean depths of mercy that are flowing full
    and free;
There are precious pearls of promise that can ne'er be
    priced in gold,
There's a fulness in my Saviour that has never yet been told.
        —J. Stuart Holden

When reading Scripture, we should be alert to discover what God has promised to do, and then we should lay hold of His promise. "The man who desires to have power with God and prevail, cannot make too sure of the pleas and promises which undergird his supplications" (H. S. Curr).[2] We shall discover promises for adversity and prosperity; promises of peace, guidance, protection, strength, deliverance, joy, and a hundred other blessings. John Bunyan made the intriguing comment that the stepping-stones of Scripture run through every Slough of Despond.

But there is a yawning gap between the vast range of God's promises and our experience of their fulfillment, simply because we have not bestirred ourselves to claim them. Are we claiming our inheritance? God assures us that we are "heirs according to the promise" (Galatians 3:29).

Think of the blessings assured in some of the great prayer promises. (1) Anything is possible that is within the will of God. "Everything is possible for one who believes" (Mark 9:23). (2) Adequate grace is available for every need. "My God will meet all your needs" (Philippians 4:19). (3) Immediate help is assured in time of need. "Before they call I will answer; while they are still speaking I will hear" (Isaiah 65:24). (4) The limitless ability of God is at our disposal. He "is able to do immeasurably more than all we ask or imagine" (Ephesians 3:20). (5) Tranquillity flows from prayer. "In every situation, by prayer and petition ... And the peace of God, which transcends all understanding, will guard your hearts and your minds in Christ Jesus" (Philippians 4:6–7).

We are not authorized to claim in prayer things that God has not promised. This seeming restriction is greatly offset by the variety and comprehensiveness of the things that He has promised. We should therefore make sure that our petitions come within the scope of what has been offered. James and John, in asking the Lord to grant them places of honor on either side of Him, were asking for something for which they had no warrant, and their request was not granted (Mark 10:35–40).

TURNING PROMISES INTO FACTS

In the practice of prayer, it is important to distinguish between promises and facts. They may often look alike, but a more careful reading will reveal an important difference. In spiritual experience, the distinction is much more than academic. Indeed, it can prove life transforming.

- We are to believe and accept as true every revealed fact of God's Word.
- We are to plead and claim the fulfillment of every promise of God's Word.

- If there is a clear statement of fact, faith accepts it without question. If there is a promise, faith fulfills any conditions that are attached and then pleads it in full confidence of its being fulfilled.
- A fact calls forth our praise.
- A promise calls for our claiming.
- The function of faith is to turn God's promises into facts.

Let us consider two examples: "Where two or three gather in my name, *there am I with them*" (Matthew 18:20, italics added). Is this a promise or a fact? It is usually treated as though it were the former. Actually, it is not a promise for us to claim but a simple assertion of fact. Jesus said, "There am I," not "There will I be, if you claim My promise." What point is there in pleading with Christ to be present when He says He is already there?

"God . . . *has blessed us* in the heavenly realms with every spiritual blessing in Christ" (Ephesians 1:3, italics added). Promise or fact? Paul does not say that God will bless us if we lay hold of the promise, but He asserts that God has already blessed us, and we have simply to believe it and to enjoy the reality of it in our experience.

Seeing the terrible aftermath of violence and suffering that followed Cambodia's fall to the Khmer Rouge in 1975, a magazine writer asked: "How does one relate this tragedy with God's promise that when He opens a door, no man is able to shut it? Has God failed?"

The answer is twofold. (1) The text quoted, "See, I have placed before you an open door that no one can shut"

(Revelation 3:8), is not a promise but a statement of fact. There is therefore no question of God's failing to keep His promise. (2) In the previous verse, the Lord had told John to write of Him that "What he opens no one can shut, *and what he shuts no one can open*" (italics added). Although no one can shut a door that God has opened, He reserves the sovereign right to shut a door Himself when His purpose has been fulfilled, and He seems to have done so in the case of Cambodia. The problem is solved when a statement of fact is differentiated from a promise.

But because He shut the door, does that mean that His purposes for Cambodia had failed? Despite the tragedy, within a few weeks of Cambodia's fall this report was received:

> Jimmy Rim, a Korean, reports that 600 Cambodians have turned to Christ in a refugee camp in Thailand. In northeast Thailand John Ellison has led over 100 refugees to Christ. Norman and Marie Ens saw 21 come to Christ recently in Bangkok. Merle Graven spoke in the Indiantown Gap Refugee Centre, and 123 Cambodians responded to the invitation. At Camp Pendleton 118 persons have accepted Christ. Andrew Way of OMF is training 170 for baptism in South Thailand. Within a period of approximately three months, about 1000 Cambodian refugees have accepted Christ.[3]

The significance of all this will be seen when it is noted that five years earlier there were only six hundred Christians in Cambodia.

Promises Must Be Claimed

The promises of God must be claimed in faith. It was "through faith" that the patriarchs "gained what was promised" (Hebrews 11:33). Often there is a condition attached to a promise. Our part is to fulfill the condition, claim the answer, and confidently wait for it. It is here that we may have to do battle with our adversary the Devil. Faith is always tested, and Satan will do all in his power to dislodge us from the plane of faith. "Satan comes and takes away the word" (Mark 4:15).

John Bunyan graphically described his experience as he endeavored to claim the promises. "Satan would labour to pull the promise from me, telling me that Christ did not mean me in John 6:37. He pulled, and I pulled. But God be praised, I got the better of him."

Our Attitude to the Promises

We can adopt one of three attitudes to God's promises:

1. We can fall short of them by devaluing them to the level of our past experience (Romans 3:23). It is possible for us so to tone them down that we come far short of what God is offering us.

2. We can stagger or waver in unbelief because the risk involved seems too great or because the promise seems too good to be true (Romans 4:20). But the one who wavers misses the blessing.

3. We can be fully persuaded and receive the promises. Abraham, the man of faith, was "fully persuaded that God had power to do what he had promised" (Romans 4:21).

The Lord has promised good to me,
His Word my hope secures;
He will my shield and portion be
As long as life endures.

—*John Newton*

With God, promise and performance are inseparable. "For no matter how many promises God has made, they are 'Yes' in Christ. And so through him the 'Amen' is spoken by us to the glory of God" (2 Corinthians 1:20).

When God makes a promise, that promise is His yes, and Jesus is the guarantee of its fulfillment. The yes is God's. "Amen" is my response of faith—my expression of confidence that the promise will be fulfilled. I say amen in the same sense when I cash a check signed by another person. It is a poor compliment if we respond to God's gracious yes with a faltering amen.

Prayer

O Lord Jesus Christ, who hast said that Thou art the way, the truth and the life; suffer us not at any time to stray from Thee, who art the way; nor to distrust the promises, which art the truth; nor to rest in any other thing but Thee, who art the life; beyond which there is nothing to be desired, neither in heaven nor on earth; for Thy Name's sake.

—Erasmus

Questions

1. Go through one of the briefer epistles and distinguish the promises from the facts in it.

2. What is taught concerning the relationship of God to His promises in the following Scriptures: Psalm 105:42; Romans 4:21; Hebrews 10:23; 2 Peter 3:9?

Seven

Discovering the Will of God

KEY TOPICS
What Is the Will of God?
How Can We Know God's Will?

God's will . . . good, pleasing . . . perfect . . .

—Romans 12:2

Our seventh lesson centers on John's assurance: "This is the confidence we have in approaching God: that if we ask anything according to his will, he hears us. And if we know that he hears us—whatever we ask—we know that we have what we asked of him" (1 John 5:14–15).

In this passage, God binds Himself to answer every prayer that comes within the scope of His will. The implications of this statement are breathtaking. Our wonder deepens when we remember that God's will is always "good, pleasing and perfect" (Romans 12:2).

But there are negative implications as well. The clause "according to his will" places a very definite limitation on the assurance of an answer. Before we endeavor to learn how to discover God's will, let us consider the will of God itself.

WHAT IS THE WILL OF GOD?

God's will is what He sovereignly purposes and plans, and as such it cannot be improved. It is perfect. Paul says that it is also "good" and "pleasing," but not every believer finds it easy to share Paul's view. The problem arises from our innate tendency to characterize what is good mainly in terms of creature comfort. We consider God's will to be good when it leads to exemption from trouble and pain, from sorrow and poverty, from bereavement and ill health, and when it makes provision for a modicum of luxury.

But such a concept finds little support in the New Testament; rather, the reverse is stated. What does Paul consider to be good? The answer is given in Romans 8:28–29: "We know that in all things God works for the good of those who love him, who have been called according to his purpose. For those God foreknew he also predestined *to be conformed to the image of his Son*" (italics added).

This often-misinterpreted passage clearly teaches that anything that makes us more like Christ is good. Christlikeness does not always thrive best in trouble-free conditions. It is more often the adverse conditions we face that most effect our transformation.

So when we "ask anything according to his will," we are really asking for what is the very best for us. The corollary is that our requests are denied only when they are against our highest interests. And would I not deny my little boy's request for a sharp razor blade, however much he cries for it? This apparent limitation to answered prayer is in effect a gracious act of love.

How Can We Know God's Will?

We face a dual problem. How can we know with certainty what is and what is not the will of God? If I do not know with certainty that my petition is in the will of God, how can I pray in faith? There must be a reasonable and satisfying answer, or God could be charged with unfairness in imposing a condition we are unable to fulfill.

It is my conviction that the answer to our questions will gradually emerge as we engage in the practice of prayer rather than while we are studying its theory. Study is, of course, necessary, but it must not be divorced from actual prayer.

True prayer is not asking God for what we want but for what He wants. This is implicit in the petition of the pattern prayer: "Your will be done on earth" (Matthew 6:10). As William Barclay remarks, it is not "Thy will be changed," but "Thy will be done." Prayer is not a convenient method of getting one's own way or of bending God to one's desires. Prayer is the means by which our desires can be redirected and aligned with the will of God. As we pray expectantly for light concerning the will of God on any matter, if our desires are not in line with His will, He will make it clear. If we are willing, He will change and redirect our desires, as Paul assures us: "It is God who works in you to will and to act in order to fulfill his good purpose" (Philippians 2:13).

We must not imagine that God will indiscriminately grant anything we desire. What would happen in the world if this were so? What chaos! The farmer prays urgently for rain to save his crops on the same day that the vacationer prays earnestly for sunshine. People in Britain pray for the success of their armies during World War II, while the Germans are praying for victory for their troops. God cannot grant both requests.

How are we to pray in such situations? Only one prayer is appropriate: "Lord, we do not know how to pray as we ought; may Thy will be done on earth in this matter as it is done in heaven." (See Romans 8:26 and Matthew 6:10.)

The supreme example of the redirection of human will in prayer is that of our Lord in Gethsemane's garden. As Son of Man, Jesus was utterly submissive to His Father's will. Yet in His humanity He shrank from the unutterable sufferings involved in His work as Mediator. In His distress He prayed, "Father, if you are willing, take this cup from me; yet not my will, but yours be done" (Luke 22:42). Had He been certain that it was the will of His Father that He accept that cup, His prayer would have been pointless. But He was not certain. He prayed to discover His Father's will, and the answer came.

In His petition we come face-to-face with the mystery of Christ's two natures. Note the "my will" and "your will." As man, He longed to be spared the agony ahead, but as He prayed, the mists surrounding His Father's will were dissolved and the issues became clear. He embraced His Father's will, His human will became merged with it, and He delighted in it.

His second prayer had no contrast between "my will" and "your will" in it. In Matthew 26:42 it is simply, "may your will be done." Then He "prayed the third time, saying the same thing" (Matthew 26:44). And what was the outcome of the three sessions of prayer? Did He induce the Father to change His mind and remove the cup? No, indeed. But in prayer the will of God became clear, and Jesus was led to accept it with exultation. Listen to the joy and the inflexible purpose of His redirected will as He speaks to Peter: "Shall I not drink the cup the Father has given me?" (John 18:11).

Amy Wilson Carmichael, founder of the Dohnavur Fellowship in India, said that early in their work they decided that before asking for anything, they should find out whether it was the mind of the Lord, although that kind of praying took time. The more they searched the Scriptures, the more they were encouraged to ask to be filled with the knowledge of His will before offering petitions for a desired benefit.

The experience of Christ in Gethsemane teaches us that prayer is not necessarily unanswered when it is not answered exactly as we would wish. It is clearly stated that the Lord's prayers were answered: "During the days of Jesus' life on earth, he offered up prayers and petitions with fervent cries and tears to the one who could save him from death, and he was heard because of his reverent submission" (Hebrews 5:7).

The answer was not what His human nature craved, but through prayers and tears He was brought to the place where He preferred and chose His Father's will and proved it to be "good, pleasing and perfect" (Romans 12:2). In our experience, as in His, sometimes it is only through tears and heartbreak that we reach the place where we can say with all our hearts, "Even so, Father: for so it seemed good in thy sight" (Matthew 11:26 KJV).

In our Lord's high-priestly prayer, however, the emphasis is different. Then He knew with full assurance that His petition was in keeping with His Father's will. He did not say, "Father, if you are willing" (Luke 22:42). Instead, He boldly prayed, "Father, I *will* that they also, whom thou hast given me, be with me where I am" (John 17:24 KJV, italics added). In matters in which the will of God is clear, we can ask with complete confidence of a full answer.

How then are we to discern the will of God in specific matters so that we can offer the prayer of faith?

1. Let us *recognize that all matters of moral and spiritual principle are dealt with clearly in the Scriptures.* In studying them, we can find in general God's will on matters of importance in our daily lives. For example, God speaks clearly on matters of morals, the marriage relationship, relationships with others, ethical behavior, social responsibility, and so on. It is our responsibility to search out what is revealed. Where the Scriptures speak clearly, we need seek no further guidance. So the first question to ask is, Is what I am asking something that is sanctioned by the Word of God?

2. In applying general principles to specific cases for which there is no clear biblical guidance, we are to *look to the Holy Spirit to teach us.* It is axiomatic that He will never guide us to ask something that is contrary to the Scriptures He has inspired. But as we pray, sincerely seeking and choosing God's will, He will restrain us from offering petitions that are not acceptable. Or, on the other hand, He will impart a deepening assurance of what God's will is in the matter.

This inner assurance then becomes the basis for the prayer of faith.

3. If we are sure our prayers are moving in the direction of God's will, we can *expect Him to add confirmation by giving indications of the divine providence in the circumstance.* A helpful example of this principle is given in the experience of Paul and his companions on the fateful missionary journey that brought them to Macedonia (Acts 16:6–10). After being twice restrained by the Holy Spirit from proceeding in a direction that was not in His plan for them, they spent some time at Troas, where they waited on God to discover His will. Since Mysia and Bithynia had both proved to be out of God's will, what were they to do?

God answered their earnest and submissive prayers by granting them a vision that was confirmed by the Holy Spirit. Luke records their reaction: "We got ready at once to leave for Macedonia, concluding [assuredly gathering, KJV] that God had called us to preach the gospel to them" (v. 10). As the missionaries moved forward in this confidence, circumstances confirmed that in their prayer they had correctly discerned the will of God.

4. *Another way God indicates His will is in laying on our hearts a special burden* for someone or some situation, from which we can find relief only in prayer. When this occurs, we may conclude that He has so burdened us because He intends to work through our prayers. He thus takes us into fellowship with Himself in the ministry of intercession.

Thomas Goodwin, the Puritan, wrote in this connection: "The Holy Spirit who is the Intercessor within us, and who searches the deep things of God, doth offer, prompt and suggest to us in our prayers those very things that are in God's heart, to grant the thing we desire of Him, so as it often comes to pass that a poor creature is carried on to speak God's very heart to Himself, and then God cannot, nor doth not deny."[1]

PRAYER

Set before our minds and hearts, O heavenly Father, the example of our Lord Jesus Christ, who when He was upon earth, found His refinement in doing the will of Him who sent Him, and in finishing His work. Give us grace to remember Him who knew neither impatience of spirit nor confusion of work, but in the midst of all His labours held communion with Thee, and even upon earth was still in heaven; where now He reigneth with Thee and the Holy Spirit, world without end.

—Dean C. J. Vaughan

QUESTIONS

1. Could God retain His sovereignty if He dispensed with the condition of answered prayer that we must ask "according to his will"?

2. Does praying in submission to the will of God hinder us from praying the prayer of faith?

Eight

The All-Powerful Name

"... anything in my name ..."

—John 14:14

I s it not significant that in His last discourse with His disciples, our Lord six times in close succession spoke of praying "in my name" (John 14:13–14; 15:16; 16:23–27)? He must surely have attached singular importance to this advanced lesson in the school of prayer. It is the view of Dr. A. T. Pierson that this truth of identity with Christ in the use of His name is the richest lesson ever taught even by the Lord Himself, and this is the theme of our eighth study.

It was a new concept to the apostles, and He endeavored to impress them with the all-prevailing power He was placing in their hands. "Until now you have not asked for anything in my name. Ask and you will receive, and your joy will be complete" (John 16:24). Henceforth their prayers were to have a new dimension, and they were to pray in a different way. As they prayed in His name, the Father would hear and answer their prayers for His sake.

In encouraging the disciples so to pray, our Lord used universal and unconditional terms concerning the level of answer they could expect—*whatever, anything*—so influential is the name of Christ. As Samuel Chadwick wrote, "Prayer reaches its highest level when offered in the Name which is above every name, for it lifts the petitioner into unity and identity with Himself."[1]

Praying in His Name

What does it mean to pray in the name of Christ? It is a striking fact that Jesus never defined what He meant by this—apparently because He assumed it would be self-evident to members of the nation to which God had entrusted the honor of His name. This is implicit, for example, in God's lament: "It is not for your sake, people of Israel, that I am going to do these things, but for the sake of my holy name, which you have profaned among the nations where you have gone" (Ezekiel 36:22).

The name stands for the person. When a name is called, we immediately envision the person bearing it. When Jesus said to His Father, "I have manifested thy name unto the men which thou gavest me" (John 17:6 kjv), He meant that He had shown them God's character—all that He is in Himself and in His relations to humans. To believe "in the name of God's one and only Son" (John 3:18) means to believe in the person of Christ, in all that He is and has done. The name stands for the person.

In this connection, Dr. H. W. Frost makes an illuminating comment:

> First, a name signifies personality, for names are given to distinguish between individuals.... Second, a name signifies a person's character, for the name which designates a person stands for what that person is.... Third, a name signifies a person's life-work, or life-history, for ... what he is represents also what he has done.... Fourth, a name signifies a person's reputation before men.... [Fifth], ... a person's name signifies the individual's standing before God, for ... [it] represents ... what he has done.[2]

Bearing these thoughts in mind, we note that the significance of the name of our Lord lies, in part, in the fact that in Scripture there are no fewer than 143 names and titles given to Him, each of which reflects light on His character and work. His is indeed a name above every name.

Is it not a staggering thought that our unique and glorious Lord has authorized us to make use of His mighty name? There is obviously infinitely greater significance in this than merely appending the formula "in Jesus' name" to our prayers, for His name enshrines not only His love but also His power.

MAKING USE OF HIS NAME

What does it mean to do something in the name of another? Does it not imply that we do it as his representative and with his power and authority? We are no longer acting in our own names or by our own authority. The Pharisee in Christ's parable came to God in his own name and pleaded his own virtues, and he went away empty (Luke 18:9–14). We have been authorized to make Christ's name the basis of our pleas. Our prayers are answered and we experience God's favor on the grounds of His merit, not our own.

A striking example of the use of another's name occurs in Esther 8:7–8. "King Xerxes replied to Queen Esther and to Mordecai the Jew. . . . 'Now write another decree in the king's name in behalf of the Jews as seems best to you, and seal it with the king's signet ring—for no document written in the king's name and sealed with his ring can be revoked.'" Is this not exactly what Christ is doing? He entrusts us with His name and gives us the signet ring of God so that what we ask in His name becomes divinely authoritative.

Therefore, when we pray in His name, it means that we present prayers that He can endorse and of which He would approve. We should pray only for things that are consistent with His name and character.

A husband entrusts his beloved wife, who is one with him in interests and purpose, with his checkbook, but he would not entrust it to an embezzler. In a similar way, Christ entrusts the use of His name to those who are in harmony with Him in His purpose and who have a community of interest with Him in seeking His Father's glory.

"To pray in the Name of Christ," said Samuel Chadwick, "is to pray as one who is at one with Christ, whose mind is the mind of Christ, whose desires are the desires of Christ, and whose purpose is one with that of Christ. . . . Prayers offered in the Name of Christ are scrutinised and sanctified by His nature, His purpose, and His will. Prayer is endorsed by the Name, when it is in harmony with the character, mind, desire, and purpose of the Name."[3]

What high honor the Master has conferred on us in giving to all His followers the use of His name at all times for all we desire—for this is what is involved in the verses we have been considering. The only limitation is on our side—that we ask only things consistent with His name and character.

Here again we are dependent on the help of the Holy Spirit to know how to use the name of Jesus aright. Instructing His disciples in the art of prayer, He said, "Until now you have not asked for anything in my name. . . . *In that day* you will ask in my name" (John 16:24, 26, italics added). In what day? The day when the Holy Spirit would be outpoured and would begin His full ministry in their lives, teaching them "all truth" (John 16:13). He would interpret to them the petitions that were consistent with the name of Christ and were therefore assured of answer.

Before He returned to heaven, Jesus committed His interests into the hands of failing and frail men. He signed a power of attorney in their favor entitling them—and us—to use His name in drawing on the bank of heaven for any needful supplies for the welfare of His work.

PRAYER

Eternal Father, who didst give Thine only Son the Name most dear to Thee and needful for mankind, betokening not His majesty but our salvation: we pray Thee to set the Name of Jesus high above every name, and to plant in every heart the love of the only Saviour, who liveth and reigneth with Thee and the Holy Spirit, one God, world without end.

—The Cambridge Bede Book

QUESTIONS

1. Praying in the Name of Jesus is to pray in union with the life and mind of Christ. What is involved in this statement?

2. Follow through the way the apostles used the powerful name of Jesus in Acts 2–4.

Praying in the Spirit

KEY TOPICS

The Spirit and the Word
Our Two Advocates
What Does It Mean to "Pray in the Spirit"?
How Does the Spirit Help Us in Prayer?

The Spirit himself intercedes for us.

—Romans 8:26

We now come to the extremely important lesson on the part played by the Holy Spirit in the prayer life of the disciple of Christ. "True prayer," wrote Samuel M. Zwemer, "is God the Holy Spirit talking to God the Father in the name of God the Son, and the believer's heart is the prayer-room."[1]

There is scriptural warrant for asserting that our chronic disinclination and our reluctance to pray, as well as our ignorance of how to pray aright, find their complete answer in the ministry of the Holy Spirit in our hearts. Hence

Paul's injunction, "And pray in the Spirit on all occasions" (Ephesians 6:18).

The Holy Spirit is the Source and Sustainer of the spiritual life. "Since we live by the Spirit, let us keep in step with the Spirit" (Galatians 5:25). Since prayer is represented in Scripture as an essential factor in progress in the Christian life, it is not surprising to find that the Spirit of God is deeply involved in this sphere.

THE SPIRIT AND THE WORD

It hardly need be said that to pray in the Spirit means to pray in harmony with *the Word of God*, which He has inspired. He does not speak with two voices. He will never move us to pray for something that is not sanctioned by Scripture.

"There is an inseparable union between the Spirit, the Word and prayer," writes H. W. Frost, "which indicates that the Spirit will always lead the saint to make much of the Word, and especially God's promises in the Word. . . . This explains the fact that the great pray-ers have always been great students of the Word."[2]

It naturally follows that praying in the Spirit means to pray in harmony with the will of God. Being God Himself, the Spirit knows and can interpret God's will to us. Indeed, this is one of the reasons why He has been given to the church. "The Spirit intercedes for God's people in accordance with the will of God" (Romans 8:27). We can count on Him to enable us to pray in harmony with the will of God.

Prayer in the Spirit is prayer whose supreme object is *the glory of God*; only in a secondary sense does it seek a blessing for self or for others. This is not natural to us, for it is our natural tendency to be more concerned with our own interests and glory. The Holy Spirit will help us in this weakness and will impart the motivation to shift our center from self to God.

Samuel Chadwick points out that the Holy Spirit never works alone; His activity is always in cooperation with human beings. "He depends upon human cooperation for the mediation of His mind, the manifestation of His truths, and the effectual working of His will.... We pray in the Spirit, and the Spirit maketh intercession for us."[3]

OUR TWO ADVOCATES

In this prayer life, believers have the aid of two Advocates who continually make themselves available and plead our causes. How rich we are through this twofold ministry! The Son of God intercedes for us before the throne of glory, securing for us the benefits of His mediatorial work. "But if anybody does sin, we have an advocate with the Father—Jesus Christ, the Righteous One" (1 John 2:1). We are thus the objects of His advocacy and intercession, which He carries on apart from us in heaven.

The Spirit of God is Christ's Advocate in our hearts to meet our deepest needs. In announcing the advent of the Holy Spirit, Jesus said, "Unless I go away, the Advocate [Helper, Counselor, or Intercessor] will not come to you; but if I go, I will send him to you" (John 16:7). "But you know him, for he lives with you and will be in you" (John 14:17). Paul gives further light on His activity in prayer: "The Spirit himself intercedes for us through wordless groans" (Romans 8:26). We are thus the vehicles of the Spirit's intercession, which He carries on within us, through our redeemed personalities. Writing on this aspect of the Spirit's ministry, Andrew Murray said,

> Just as wonderful and real is the divine work of God on the throne graciously hearing, and by His mighty power, answering prayer. Just as divine as is the work of the Son, interceding and securing and transmitting the answer from above, is the work of the Holy Spirit in us in the prayer that awaits and obtains the answer. The intercession within is as divine as the intercession above.[4]

Weakness and inadequacy in the art of prayer are not surprising to God. He never intended that prayer should be left to our own unaided faculties. So He gave the Holy Spirit to instruct, inspire, and illumine our hearts and minds. Unaided by Him, we would be likely to pray for things not only contrary to God's will, but injurious to ourselves.

What Does It Mean to "Pray in the Spirit"?

We must first understand the meaning of the phrase "in the Spirit." H. C. G. Moule interprets it as meaning "surrounded by His presence and power": "The Holy Spirit was to be 'the Place' of the prayer, in the sense of being the surrounding, penetrating, transforming atmosphere of the spirit of the praying Christian."[5]

Kenneth Wuest points out that "in the Spirit" is locative of sphere. That is, all true prayer is exercised in the sphere of the Holy Spirit, motivated and empowered by Him. The expression "praying in the Holy Spirit" also states the means of prayer. We pray by means of the Holy Spirit, in dependence on Him.[6]

It is clear that praying in the Spirit means much more than praying with the Spirit's help, although that is included. We pray by means of and in dependence on the Spirit's help, but the Spirit is the atmosphere in which the believer lives. So long as He is not grieved, He is able to guide us in our petitions and create in us the faith that claims the answer. Our prayers will then be in substance the same as the intercessions of the Spirit within.

So, praying in the Spirit is praying along the same lines, about the same things, and in the same name as the Holy Spirit is.

How Does the Spirit Help Us in Prayer?

1. It is He who introduces us into the presence of the Father. "For through him we ... have access to the Father by one Spirit" (Ephesians 2:18). The picture behind *access* is that of a court official introducing people who desire an audience with the king. This is exactly what the Spirit does for us.

2. As the "spirit of grace and supplication" (Zechariah 12:10), He overcomes our reluctance, working in us the desire to pray. He graciously, yet faithfully, reveals to us our true heart-needs, and He leads us to seek their fulfillment in prayer.

3. He imparts a sense of sonship and acceptance that creates freedom and confidence in the presence of God. "God sent the Spirit of his Son into our hearts, the Spirit who calls out, 'Abba! Father!'" (Galatians 4:6). Children are uninhibited in the presence of an understanding and loving father, and so may we be in our prayers.

4. He helps us in the ignorance of our minds and in the infirmities of our bodies, as well as in the maladies of the soul. "In the same way, the Spirit helps us in our weakness. We do not know what we ought to pray for" (Romans 8:26), or as it is in the King James Version, "We know not what we should pray for as we ought."

We can count on the Spirit's aid in guiding us into the will of God by illumining Scripture to us and by stimulating and directing our mental processes. He purifies our desires and redirects them toward the will of God, for He alone knows and can interpret God's will and purpose. "No one knows the thoughts of God except the Spirit of God" (1 Corinthians 2:11). He also improves our motivation and inspires confidence and faith in a loving Father.

5. He takes our faltering and imperfect prayers, adds to them the incense of the merits of Christ, and puts them in a form acceptable to our heavenly Father. "Another angel, who had a golden censer, came and stood at the altar. He was given much incense to offer, with the prayers of all God's people, on the golden altar in front of the throne" (Revelation 8:3). He takes our inarticulate groanings and infuses the right meaning into them.

6. He lays special burdens of prayer on the believer who is walking sensitively in companionship with Him. Such burdens,

intolerable at times, were laid on the prophets; often they could get relief only through prolonged and earnest prayer.

Daniel 10:2–3 refers to one such experience: "At that time I, Daniel, mourned for three weeks. I ate no choice food; no meat or wine touched my lips; and I used no lotions at all until the three weeks were over." But the answer came at the proper time—God's time.

When He lays such prayer burdens on the hearts of His children, He intends to answer the prayer through their intercessions. He will impart the strength to pray through until the answer comes.

The foregoing considerations would lead us to conclude that to be able to pray prevailingly, we must be filled with the Holy Spirit. "We are never really men of prayer in the best sense, until we are filled with the Holy Spirit." This necessity is emphasized by J. Stuart Holden in a passage cited by E. M. Bounds:

> Here is the secret of prevailing prayer, to pray under a direct inspiration of the Holy Spirit, whose petitions for us and through us are always according to the Divine purpose, and hence certain of answer. "Praying in the Holy Ghost is but co-operating with the will of God, and such prayer is always victorious. How many Christians there are who cannot pray, and who seek by effort, resolve, joining prayer circles, etc., to cultivate in themselves the 'holy art of intercession,' and all to no purpose. Here for them and for all is the only secret of a real prayer life—'Be filled with the Spirit,' who is 'the Spirit of grace and supplication.'"[7]

The prayers I make will then be sweet indeed
If Thou the Spirit give by which I pray:
My unassisted heart is barren clay,
That of its nature self can nothing feed;
Of good and pious works Thou art the seed,
That quickens only when Thou say'st it may;
Unless Thou show to us Thine own true way
No man can find it: Father! Thou must lead.

—*Michelangelo*

PRAYER

O Holy Spirit, Giver of light and life, impart to us thoughts higher than our own thoughts and prayers better than our own prayers and powers beyond our own powers, that we may spend and be spent in the ways of love and goodness, after the perfect image of our Lord and Savior, Jesus Christ.

—Anonymous

QUESTIONS

1. What does Romans 8:26–27 teach about the part played by God the Father and God the Spirit in the prayer life of the believer?

2. In what ways does being filled with the Spirit improve the quality of one's prayer life?

Ten

The Prayer of Faith

KEY TOPICS
The Basis of the Prayer of Faith
How Can We Be Sure?
A Staggeringly Inclusive Promise

"Have faith in God."

—Mark 11:22

We come now to a spiritual principle of overriding importance in relation to answered prayer. It is enunciated in Hebrews 11:6: "And without faith it is *impossible* to please God, because anyone who comes to him *must believe* that he exists and that he rewards those who earnestly seek him" (italics added). There is no acceptable substitute for faith. Faith feeds on the pledged Word of God and flourishes in the atmosphere of His presence.

It has been said that just as there are two pairs of eyes, natural eyes and spiritual eyes, so there are two kinds of faith, natural faith and spiritual faith. Natural faith is common to us all and is the basis of community life. We post a letter in the faith that the postal authorities will deliver it to the addressee, and our faith is usually rewarded. Business also runs on the basis of natural faith.

Both natural and spiritual faith must have a sufficient foundation. If I had no faith in the postal system, I would not pay out the money to post a letter. The faith of the business professional making transactions rests on the moral integrity and financial resources of his or her client. But spiritual faith is the possession only of Christians. It views things through spiritual eyes and perceives things invisible to the natural eye. Faith is the substance of, the substantiating of, the giving substance to things not seen (Hebrews 11:1). Such faith is not inherent in human nature but is a gift of God's grace (Ephesians 2:8).

The Basis of the Prayer of Faith

What, then, constitutes an adequate basis for the prayer of faith?

On the negative side, it is not the evidence of outward circumstances. The prayer of faith often finds its grandest opportunity in the utterly impossible situation, in the absence of any tangible encouragement to believe. Elijah's prayer of faith for rain triumphed in spite of the six-times-repeated report from his servant that the sky remained cloudless (1 Kings 18:41–45). Faith does not require external confirmation but believes God in spite of appearances.

Nor does faith require or demand a sign to shore it up. Christians sometimes speak of putting out a fleece, as Gideon did, to determine what is the will of God. But was not God's response to Gideon's twice-repeated request a gracious concession to the feebleness of his faith rather than a reward for its strength (Judges 6:36–40)? Jesus constantly deprecated the seeking of a sign.

Thomas refused to be satisfied that the Lord had really risen from the dead apart from the evidence of his own senses. To him Jesus gave the gentle yet encouraging rebuke: "Because you have seen me, you have believed; blessed are those who have not seen and yet have believed" (John 20:29).

Nor do our feelings and emotional reactions constitute an adequate basis for the prayer of faith. When we instruct individuals seeking salvation, we are careful to point out that they are assured of salvation not because they feel saved but because they repose their faith in the Savior; faith is independent of feelings. Feelings are no more a basis of faith for the believer than for the unbeliever. Faith trusts God despite the absence or the contradiction of feelings.

On the positive side, the prayer of faith finds its warrant in the promises of the Word of God, applied to our hearts by the Spirit of God. It is a divinely given intuition and assurance that God has answered our prayers and granted our requests. It is not the outcome of trying to believe but is effortless confidence in God. When a husband and wife are deeply in love, it is no effort for them to trust each other.

How Can We Be Sure?

But how are we to distinguish between mere natural desires and the prompting of the Holy Spirit? John comes to our assistance on this point: "This is the confidence we have in approaching God: that if we ask anything according to his will, he hears us. And if we know that he hears us—whatever we ask—*we know that we have what we asked of him*" (1 John 5:14–15, italics added). This is one of the key verses relating to our subject.

We must first satisfy ourselves that the request is in harmony with the will of God. Once we are sure of this, we know that He hears us, because we believe Him to be true to His pledged word. That being so, John says we know that we have—not will have, but have—obtained the request. The actual enjoyment of the prayed-for blessing may be in the future, but faith regards it as already in possession.

A man who lived in a New Zealand city had a son who, in spite of a godly upbringing, was quite unresponsive to the gospel message. The father had prayed most earnestly for his son's salvation but had seen no change in his lifestyle or attitude to God. Suddenly the son was killed in an accident. The father was naturally distressed at the untimely death of his son, but with quiet assurance he told sympathizing friends that he was confident he and his son would meet in heaven—and this in spite of any evidence to support his belief.

A few weeks later, a young man came to visit the father. The young man had known the son. "We will meet your son in heaven," he said.

"Yes, I am sure of that," replied the father. "God has given me that assurance."

"Oh, I know more than that," was the reply. "A week before he was killed, we attended an evangelistic service conducted by Herbert Booth, son of the founder of the Salvation

Army. When an invitation to accept Christ was given, your son went forward, and I accompanied him."

The reply of the father to this astonishing piece of news was, "Of course I am delighted to hear what you tell me, but I am no more sure now that we shall meet in heaven than I was before you told me."[1]

Faith believes that it has received the answer, even in the absence of any confirmatory evidence.

A STAGGERINGLY INCLUSIVE PROMISE

The parallel promise of Mark 11:24 seems so staggeringly universal and inclusive in its implications that our innate unbelief causes us to feel that it surely cannot mean just what it says: "Whatever [what things soever, KJV] you ask for in prayer, believe that you *have received* it, and it will be yours" (italics added). Our natural tendency is to tone the statement down somewhat so as to bring it into the realm of the reasonable or probable. Can it really mean that if I want something all I need to do is pray and ask?

The answer is that "whatever" and "what things soever" mean exactly what they say, but in the second clause of the verse there is a limitation implied—not on God's side but on ours. For it is impossible for a believer to exercise faith for something that is beyond the scope of the will of God. If faith is the gift of God, and it is, He will not give it to someone in order to encourage the person to do something contrary to His will.

The praying Christian will be able to believe all that is sanctioned by the Word of God and witnessed to by the

Spirit. Our faith will flow from our praying. It is in the atmosphere of prayer that the Holy Spirit nurtures and develops our faith or, on the other hand, indicates to us that what we desire is contrary to God's will.

In Mrs. Hudson Taylor's *Behind the Ranges*, James O. Fraser of Lisuland recounts his experience as he learned the possibilities and potency of the prayer of faith:

> "The prayer of faith" [is] a definite request . . . made in definite faith for a definite answer. . . .
>
> In my own case here . . . I have definitely asked the Lord for several hundred families of Lisu believers. There are upwards of two thousand Lisu families in the district altogether. It might be said, "Why do you not ask for a thousand?" I answer quite frankly, because I have not faith for a thousand. . . .
>
> I prayed continually for the Tengyueh Lisu for over four years, asking many times that several hundreds of families might be turned to God. This was only general prayer, however. God was dealing with me in the meantime. . . . Then near the end of November (1914), . . . this same petition came to me as a definite burden. . . .
>
> I recognized the burden clearly. And it was an actual burden: it burdened me. I went to my room alone one afternoon and knelt in prayer. I knew that the time had come for the prayer of faith. And then, fully knowing what I was doing and what it might cost me, I definitely committed myself to this petition in faith. I "cast my burden upon the Lord."

I rose from my knees with the deep, restful conviction that I had already received the answer.... And since then (nearly a year ago now) I have never had anything but peace and joy ... in holding to the ground already claimed and taken. I have never repeated the request and never will: there is no need.... The past can never be undone, never need be redone. It is a solemn thing to enter into a faith-covenant with God. It is binding on both parties. You lift up your hand to God; ... you definitely ask for and definitely receive His proffered gift; then do not go back on your faith, even if you live to be a hundred.[2]

When Fraser wrote those words, the answer was still in the future; but in God's time a glorious answer was given and thousands of Lisu turned to the Lord. Was his stand of faith contested? Hear his further testimony:

We often have to strive and wrestle in prayer ... before we attain this quiet, restful faith.... However, once we attain to a real faith, all the forces of hell are impotent to annul it. What then? They retire and muster their forces on this plot of ground which God has pledged Himself to give us, and contest every inch of it. The real battle begins when the prayer of faith has been offered. But, praise the Lord! We are on the winning side. Let us read and re-read the tenth chapter of Joshua and never talk about defeat again.[3]

The victories won by prayer,
By prayer must still be held;
The foe retreats, but only when
By prayer he is compelled.

—Anonymous

It is worthy of note that three important factors were involved in Elijah's prevailing prayer. (1) He based his prayer on a definite promise of God (1 Kings 18:1). (2) He fulfilled the condition attached to the promise (18:2). (3) He persevered in the prayer of faith in spite of the adverse report brought by sight (18:43). "Seven times Elijah said, 'Go back,'" to his servant who brought the report. Note the progression: "There is nothing there." "A cloud as small as a man's hand is rising from the sea" (18:44). "A heavy rain started falling" (18:45). James assures us that Elijah's prayer is a model prayer of faith (James 5:16–18).

Another classic example of the prayer of faith is recounted in *The Diary of George Mueller*:

This is, perhaps, of all days the most remarkable so far as regards the funds. When I was in prayer this morning respecting them, I was enabled firmly to believe that the Lord would send help, though all seemed dark as to natural appearances. At twelve o'clock I met as usual with the brethren and sisters in prayer. There had come in only one shilling which, except twopence, had already been spent because of the great need.... Neither in the Infants' nor Boys' Orphan houses was there bread enough for tea, nor money to buy milk. Lower we had never been, perhaps never so low. We gave ourselves now unitedly to prayer, laying the case in simplicity before the Lord.... We continued for a while silently in prayer.... At last we rose from our knees. I said, "God will surely send help." The words had not quite passed my lips when I saw a letter lying on the table which had been brought while we were in prayer. It was from my wife, containing another letter with £10 for the orphans. The prayer of faith had its reward.[4]

Isabel Kuhn tells how she and her husband were experiencing great opposition in a heathen village in South China. The people were deeply convicted but could not break from their sinful customs. Then something happened.

"The last two days, without any explanation that we could discover, a sudden and astounding change took place," she wrote. Glorious victories were gained and quarrels settled. They did not know it, but a letter giving the explanation was already on the way. She had noted the date in her diary and said to her husband, "I am sure someone in the homelands is specially praying for us." Two months passed, and then a letter. "John," she said, "you read this while I get my diary." This is what he read:

I must write and tell you what happened today. All morning I could not do my housework because of the burden on me concerning Three Clan Village. So finally I went to the telephone and called Mrs. W. She said she had been feeling the same way and suggested we call Mrs. J. and all go to prayer together. We did so, each in her own kitchen. We spent the morning in intercession for three quarrelling clans. We feel God has answered. You will know?

The date in the diary corresponded exactly with the victory gained in Three Clan Village.

Let us conclude by recapitulating the words of Hudson Taylor: "Faith is reliance on the trustworthiness of those with whom we transact business. Our faith is the recognition of God's faithfulness. It is so blessed to leave our faith out of account, and to be so occupied with God's faithfulness that we cannot raise any question whatsoever."

PRAYER

Blessed Jesus, it is Thyself in whom our faith must be rooted if it is to grow strong. Thy work has freed us from the power of sin and opened the way to the Father; Thy Spirit is always drawing us upward into a life of perfect faith and confidence; we are assured that in Thy teaching we shall learn to pray the prayer of faith. Thou wilt train us to pray so that we believe that we receive, to believe that we really have what we ask. Lord, teach me so to love and trust Thee that my soul may have in Thee assurance that I am heard.

—Anonymous

QUESTIONS

1. If the Holy Spirit has been grieved in our lives, what effect would that have on our ability to pray the prayer of faith? What should we do?

2. How can our faith be increased so that we can ask God confidently for larger answers?

❧ *Eleven* ❧

Shameless Persistence

KEY TOPICS
The Three Friends
The Unprincipled Judge
Why Is Importunity Necessary?
"An Athletic of the Soul"
Our Part Not Yet Fully Done
Two Importunate Intercessors

"... because of his importunity ..."

—Luke 11:8 KJV

We come now to a requirement in prayer that is rather surprising, and to some, not a little puzzling. It seems that God is moved to answer our prayers in response to a persistence that will not take no for an answer— "shameless persistence," someone has rendered it.

Jesus employed varied methods in imparting truth to His disciples. Sometimes He used paradox, sometimes parable. In some parables truth was taught by comparison, in others,

93

by contrast. He adopted the latter in telling two parables that enforce the necessity of importunity and perseverance in prayer.

THE THREE FRIENDS (LUKE 11:5–8)

There are three persons in this parable—the one spoken for, the one who speaks, and the one appealed to. The Lord vividly contrasts the reluctance and selfishness of the friend appealed to with the openhanded and openhearted generosity of the heavenly Father. The man appealed to was not concerned about his friend's distress. The argument runs: If even a self-centered and ungenerous human being, to whom sleep is more important than his friend's distress and need, will reluctantly rise at midnight to supply the need because of his friend's shameless persistence, how much more will God be moved by persistent entreaty to meet His children's needs! "Though he will not get up and give you the bread because of friendship, yet because of your shameless audacity he will surely get up and give you as much as you need" (v. 8).

THE UNPRINCIPLED JUDGE (LUKE 18:1–8)

The parable of the heartless and unprincipled judge, who has neither reverence for God nor respect for people, teaches the same lesson even more strongly. If the defenseless but troublesome widow by her shameless persistence can overcome the reluctance of the unjust judge to do her justice, how much more will the believer be speedily vindicated in the court of heaven, where we have a strong Advocate whose character is the exact opposite of the judge's? "And will not God bring about justice for his chosen ones, who cry out to him day and night? Will he keep putting them off? I tell you, he will see that they get justice, and quickly" (vv. 7–8).

In both parables, Jesus is careful to vindicate the character of God and to reveal His true nature and attitude. "If you, then, though you are evil, know how to give good gifts to your children, *how much more* will your Father in heaven give good gifts to those who ask him!" (Matthew 7:11, italics added). God is neither a selfish neighbor nor a crooked judge dispensing reluctant justice to a wronged widow simply because his comfort is disturbed by her persistence.

The lesson is that lukewarmness in prayer, as in everything else, is nauseating to God and comes away empty-handed. On the other hand, shameless persistence, the importunity that will not be denied, returns with the answer in its hands.

Do our prayers lack urgency? Can we do without the thing for which we are asking? Or is it something we must have at all costs? John Knox cried, "Give me Scotland or I die." The saint and patriot would not be denied. Jesus encourages us to believe that this is the kind of praying that receives an answer. Importunity is an important element in answered prayer.

Adoniram Judson, the great missionary to Burma, was a man of prayer. He said,

> God loves importunate prayer so much that He will not give us much blessing without it. And the reason He loves such prayer is that He loves us, and knows that it is a necessary preparation for our receiving the richest blessing He is waiting and longing to bestow.

I never prayed sincerely and earnestly for anything but it came at some time—no matter at how distant a day, somehow, in some shape, probably the last I would have devised, it came.[1]

WHY IS IMPORTUNITY NECESSARY?

Since God is a loving heavenly Father who knows all our needs better than we do, why should He require us to importune Him? Why does He not just grant our requests, as He is well able to do?

This is something of a mystery, and the answer does not appear on the surface. We can be assured that there is no reluctance on God's part to give us whatever is good for us. He does not need to be coaxed, for He is not capricious. Prayer is not a means of extorting blessing from unwilling fingers. The "how much more" of Matthew 7:11 affirms this with emphasis. The answer must be sought elsewhere. The necessity must lie in us, not in God. It is not God who is under test but our own spiritual maturity.

Dr. W. E. Biederwolf makes the interesting suggestion that importunity is one of the instructors in God's training school for Christian culture. It may be that God does not grant the answer to a prayer at once because the petitioner is not yet in a fit state to receive what he or she asks. There is something God desires to do in the believer before He answers the prayer. There may be some lack of yieldedness or some failure to master some previous spiritual lesson. So while He does not deny the request, He withholds the answer until, through persevering prayer, the end He has in view is achieved.

May this not explain in part some of God's seeming delays? His delays are always delays of love, not of caprice. "Men would pluck their mercies green; God would have them ripe."

"AN ATHLETIC OF THE SOUL"

Canon W. Hay Aitken refers to prayer as "an athletic of the soul" that is designed to render our desires more intense by giving them adequate expression, to exercise the will in its highest functions, and to bring us into closer touch with God. Prayer will also test the reality and sincerity of our faith and will save it from being superficial. Importunity rouses the slumbering capacities of the soul and prepares the way for faith.[2]

There may be other reasons why the divine response tarries and importunity is needed. Here are some suggestions.

1. We may be asking without caring greatly about the issue. If we are not in earnest, why should God bestir Himself? We shall find Him when we seek with all our hearts.

2. We may be asking for selfish reasons, and the discipline of delay is necessary to purge us of this. Selfish motivation is self-defeating in prayer.

3. We may unconsciously be unwilling to pay the price involved in the answering of our prayers, and our Father desires us to face up to this fact.

4. We may be misinterpreting what God is doing in our lives in answer to our prayers. This was true of John Newton, the converted slave trader. He gives his testimony in verse:

I asked the Lord, that I may grow
In faith, and love, and every grace;
Might more of his salvation know,
And seek more earnestly his face. . . .

I hoped that in some favoured hour,
At once he'd answer my request;
And by his love's constraining power,
Subdue my sins, and give me rest.

Instead of this, he made me feel
The hidden evils of my heart;
And let the angry powers of hell
Assault my soul in every part.

Yea more, with his own hand he seemed
Intent to aggravate my woe;
Crossed all the fair designs I schemed,
Blasted my gourds, and laid me low.

Lord, why is this, I trembling cried,
Wilt thou pursue thy worm to death?
" 'Tis in this way," the Lord replied,
"I answer prayer for grace and faith.

"These inward trials I employ,
From self and pride to set thee free;
And break thy schemes of earthly joy,
That thou mayst seek thy all in me."

God's dual method with His servant was to reveal to him the inherent evil of his heart so that he would be motivated to claim importunately from God the blessing he was then fitted to receive.

5. Another possible reason for God's apparent delay or denial of an answer is put forward by Dr. D. M. McIntyre: it secures our humble dependence on God.[3] If He bestowed our desires as gifts of nature and did not want our solicitations, we would tend to become independent of Him. "You may say to yourself, 'My power and the strength of my hands have produced this wealth for me,' " was God's warning to His people. "But remember the LORD your God, for it is he who gives you the ability to produce wealth" (Deuteronomy 8:17–18).

OUR PART NOT YET FULLY DONE

For our encouragement we should remember that the walls of Jericho did not fall until the Israelites had circled them a full thirteen times and then shouted the shout of faith (Joshua 6:1–20). We may have circled our prayer-Jericho the full thirteen times, and yet the answer has not come. Why? Could it be that God is waiting to hear the shout of faith? Perhaps that is the reason the forbidding walls are still intact. He delights to see us step out in faith upon His naked promise.

> Unanswered yet? Nay, do not say unanswered,
> Perhaps your part is not yet wholly done,
> The work began when first your prayer was uttered,
> And God will finish what He has begun.
> Keep incense burning at the shrine of prayer,

And glory shall descend sometime, somewhere.
Unanswered yet? Faith cannot be unanswered;
Her feet are firmly planted on the Rock;
Amid the wildest storms she stands undaunted,
Nor quails before the loudest thunder shock.
She knows Omnipotence has heard her prayer,
And cries, "It shall be done sometime, somewhere."

—*Ophelia Guyon Browning*

Two Importunate Intercessors

Abraham and Elijah stand in contrast in two prayer engagements. In his intercession for Sodom, Abraham almost prevailed, but he failed to receive the complete answer because of failure in importunity (Genesis 18:16–33). Elijah, on the other hand, in his prayer for rain on Mount Carmel, experienced an overflowing answer (1 Kings 18:42–45). The reason is instructive.

Abraham was an intimate friend of God. In one of his conversations with God, God revealed to him the impending judgment on Sodom. Abraham interceded for his nephew Lot and the people of Sodom in a prayer of mixed argument, audacity, and humility.

It was a most remarkable prayer. Time and again Abraham enlarged his demand—fifty righteous, forty-five, forty, thirty, twenty, ten—and then he stopped praying. There was no reason to suppose God's mercy was exhausted. But while Abraham received a partial answer and Lot was delivered, Sodom was destroyed. His intercession was unsuccessful because of failure in importunity.

Elijah pressed his suit on behalf of his drought-stricken nation and refused to take no for an answer. Seven times, strong in faith, he pleaded with God, and the full answer came.

Is it without significance that Elijah prayed seven times— the number of perfection and fullness—while Abraham stopped at six times, the number of human frailty? Abraham stopped asking before God stopped answering. Let us become seven-times pray-ers.

> Faith, mighty faith the promise sees,
> And looks to God alone;
> Laughs at impossibilities,
> And cries, It shall be done!

—*C. Wesley*

PRAYER

Eternal God, who tarriest oft beyond the time we hope for but not beyond the time appointed by Thee; from which cometh from Thee the truth that cannot lie, the counsel that cannot fail. Make us faithful to stand upon our watch-tower and to wait for what Thou wilt say to us, that by our faith we may live and at the last behold Thy righteousness prevail, to the glory of Thy name.

—Anonymous

QUESTIONS

1. How can the idea of importunity be reconciled with submission to the will of God?

2. Can you think of other reasons God requires us to be importunate in prayer?

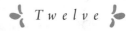

A Postmortem on Unanswered Prayer

KEY TOPIC

Possible Reasons for Failure in Prayer

... because you ask with wrong motives ...

—James 4:3

Having considered some of the most important conditions leading to answered prayer, we come face-to-face with the fact that too many of our prayers go unanswered. This is a melancholy admission in view of the multiplicity of promises God has made to the praying soul.

When prudent business managers discover that a business is running at a loss, they take stock, draw up a balance sheet, discover why they have made no profit, and take remedial steps. Shall we be less prudent in our spiritual accounting? Have we ever sat down and faced this question honestly? Do we just accept the failure of some of our prayers fatalistically? Do we piously say, "Perhaps it was not God's will after all"? Or do we ask honest questions:

- Am I sure my request was in harmony with God's will?
- Did I really pray making use of Jesus' name?
- Did I pray the prayer of faith and really expect the answer?
- Was I praying from selfish motives?
- Have I been importunate?
- Did I depend on the Holy Spirit in my praying?

I am certain that God is more honored when we honestly face and confess our failures in prayer than when we piously ignore them. So let us conduct a postmortem, search out the causes of defeat, and remedy them. When we do this sincerely, we will experience an upgrading in the quality of our prayer lives. Behind every unanswered prayer is a reason, which we must discover for ourselves.

The apostle James asserts that the basic reason for every unanswered prayer is that in some way we have asked wrongly. "When you ask, you do not receive, because you ask with wrong motives" (James 4:3). There are other reasons for unanswered prayer as well, and it is now our objective to examine these potential causes of failure.

Possible Reasons for Failure in Prayer

Eight possible explanations for failure in prayer come to mind:

1. *Perhaps our faith has been resting on the wrong foundation.* Could it be that we have been unconsciously substituting faith in prayer for faith in God? Have we been expecting our prayers to give the answer? Think this through carefully. We are nowhere in Scripture exhorted to put our faith in prayer, but we are commanded, "Have faith in God"

(Mark 11:22). If our faith is directed toward and reposes in the God to whom we pray, our faith will not stumble even if He does not do exactly what we ask. In spite of the popular motto, it is not prayer that changes things but God who changes things when we conform to His requirements for answered prayer.

Or could it be that we have been unconsciously substituting faith in our *faith* for faith in God? This may sound trite, but it is a very real possibility. When we say, "My faith is so small; I can't believe that God will do it," are we not admitting that we are depending on the quantity of our faith rather than resting on the faithful God for the answer?

It is true that "without faith it is impossible to please God" (Hebrews 11:6), but faith is like eyesight. Neither faith nor eyesight exists apart from the objects on which they are focused. Have you ever seen eyesight? There is likewise no such thing as faith in the abstract. I am to focus my faith on God and not to have faith in my faith.

Or could it be that I have been relying on my earnestness and importunity in prayer to bring the answer, instead of relying on God Himself?

2. *There may be in our hearts a secret sympathy with sin.* If this is the case, our prayers will be effectually short-circuited and our prayer lives sabotaged.

In this connection, no statement could be more explicit than Psalm 66:18: "If I had cherished sin in my heart, the Lord would not have listened." It is important to notice that the word expressed here in the New International Version as *cherished* and sometimes translated as *regarded* does not merely mean "to look on," but "to hold on to or cling to."

The psalmist was enunciating a clear spiritual principle. He claimed that he was not holding on to sin in his heart and so could testify, "but God has surely listened and has heard my prayer" (Psalm 66:19). If we are to expect an answer to our prayers, we must make a clean break with sin.

3. *Perhaps the motive behind our prayers is not pure.* "When you ask, you do not receive, because you ask with wrong motives, that you may spend what you get on your pleasures" (James 4:3).

God nowhere binds Himself to answer self-centered or selfish prayers. While He promises to meet all our genuine needs, He does not undertake to gratify all our selfish desires. In prayer for temporal things, we should examine our motivation carefully and ask, "Is this petition for God's glory, for my good, and for the good of others, or is it merely to gratify my own selfish desires?"

4. *Instead of having confidence in approaching God, we are possibly being held back by a condemning heart.* John the apostle assured those to whom he was writing that whatever condemns us in our conscience hinders prayer. Until known sin is judged and renounced, we pray and plead in vain. "Dear friends, if our hearts do not condemn us, we have confidence before God and receive from him anything we ask" (1 John 3:21–22).

If I know of some reason my conscience condemns me, I should deal with it and do all in my power to put it right with God and other people. Until I do, I will endeavor in vain to pray the prayer of faith. More often than not, this is why we are unable to exercise appropriating faith when we pray.

What are we to do if some subtle sense of guilt and condemnation descends on our spirits? We examine our hearts but can assign no reason for the distress. We experience a nameless and ill-defined depression of spirit, a vague malaise that prevents the soul from rising to God in the prayer of faith. How is this condition to be met?

First, let us sincerely ask God to reveal to us if there is some real but unrecognized sin that lies at the root of this sense of condemnation. If He reveals something to us, let us put it right at the first opportunity. Confidence toward God will thus be restored, and our prayers will receive their answers.

But should there be no such revelation of sin, we are justified in concluding that the obscuring cloud originates in enemy territory. Many have found it helpful to pray in such circumstances, "Lord, if this sense of condemnation comes from Your Spirit's conviction, make my sin clear to me and I shall confess and put it right. But if it comes from Satan, then on the grounds of Calvary's victory, I refuse and reject it."

This attitude of acceptance of the divine dealing but rejection of the satanic intrusion has often brought deliverance and renewed freedom in prayer, for it is true that "if our hearts do not condemn us, we have confidence before God."

5. *We may be entertaining bitter or unforgiving spirits.* Jesus handled this possibility very faithfully. "Therefore I tell you, whatever you ask for in prayer, believe that you have received it, and it will be yours. *And when you stand praying,* if you hold anything against anyone, *forgive them,* so that your Father in heaven may forgive you your sins" (Mark 11:24–25, italics added).

These sobering words should convince us of the folly of expecting an answer to our prayers when we are cherishing unforgiving spirits. Because I have been forgiven, I must forgive. If I fail to do so, I will be unable to pray with assurance of an answer.

Dr. H. A. Ironside told of a man who gave this testimony:

> For years I prayed for the conversion of an erring son, but all the time he seemed to go from bad to worse. During those years I had a bitter feeling in my heart towards a brother who, I felt, had grievously wronged me. I insisted upon reparation which he refused to make. Feeling my cause was just, I held this against him, and would not overlook it.
>
> At last I realized that this was hindering prayer; I judged it before God and freely forgave. O the liberty as I then turned to God about my son! Soon I heard with joy of his conversion. Though far from home, he was brought under the power of the gospel and led to Christ. An unforgiving spirit explains why thousands of petitions go apparently unheeded.[1]

6. *Perhaps all is not right in the marital relationship.* This possibility is plainly envisaged in 1 Peter 3:1–7, a passage that illumines the relationship that should exist between husband and wife and the duties they owe to one another. The paragraph begins, "Wives, in the same way submit yourselves to your own husbands," and concludes, "Husbands, in the same way be considerate as you live with your wives, and treat them with respect as the weaker partner and as heirs with you

of the gracious gift of life, *so that nothing will hinder your prayers*" (italics added).

When husband and wife are one in heart and purpose, mutually recognizing the place assigned to each in Scripture and practicing the law of love, prayer is easy and confident. But when there is a lack of that mutuality, when there is self-ishness in the intimate things of the marriage relationship, the prayer life of the couple becomes the first casualty. There may be a form of prayer maintained, but joy and spontaneity will depart and answers will be few.

When a growing family has daily evidence of such a lack of harmony and sympathy between its parents, that need can prove in itself a tragic hindrance to the answer of parental prayers. On the other hand, when the family has daily evidence of mutual and sacrificial love, the way is open for the Spirit to work and for the prayers of the parents to be answered.

7. *Our prayers are sometimes an outlet for unbelief and despair rather than for the outpouring of faith.* A fundamental prayer principle is given in Hebrews 11:6. Its absoluteness is impressive. "And without faith it is impossible to please God, because anyone who comes to him must believe that he exists and that he rewards those who earnestly seek him."

It is true that God invites us to pour out our hearts before Him and to unload our burdens at His feet. But we are to come to Him in the confidence of faith, not in the numbness of despair. Our God loves to be trusted. "But when you ask, you must believe and not doubt," exhorts James, "because the one who doubts is like a wave of the sea, blown and tossed by the wind. That person should not expect to receive anything from the Lord" (James 1:6–7).

One characteristic of a wave is that it never stays in the same place for two seconds. So it is with the unstable, double-minded, unbelieving individual, says James (v. 8). Such people put their burdens or problems in God's hands one minute and take them back again the next, only to repeat the futile process. They believe one minute and doubt the next.

The psalmist, confident in the trustworthiness of his God, has a satisfying prescription for such a person: "Commit [and leave committed] your way to the LORD; trust [and keep on trusting] in him and he will do this. . . . Be still before the LORD and wait patiently for him" (Psalm 37:5, 7).

8. *Perhaps satanic resistance that prevents the answer to our prayers from reaching us must be dealt with.* This was the experience of the prophet Daniel as recorded in Daniel 10:12–13:

> Then he continued, "Do not be afraid, Daniel. Since the first day that you set your mind to gain understanding and to humble yourself before your God, your words were heard, and I have come in response to them. But the prince of the Persian kingdom resisted me twenty-one days. Then Michael, one of the chief princes, came to help me, because I was detained there with the king of Persia."

The messenger whom God had dispatched in answer to Daniel's prayer was detained on the way for three weeks! It was only through the help of Michael, the archangel, that there had been a successful completion of his mission.

We should recognize that unseen forces rule the world. In this instance there was conflict between the spiritual forces behind the kings of Persia and the messengers from God. This is an area of truth of which we know little, but it does throw light on the mystery of unanswered prayer.

The answer to Daniel's prayer began in the heavenly sphere before it was evident on earth (v. 12). Satan, as always, opposed the purpose of God, but he did not succeed. Daniel was mystified by God's delay in answering his prayers, and it was only after he had persevered in prayer that he learned the real reason for the delay. It was not that his prayers had not been heard but that they had triggered a conflict in the heavenly realm. That conflict was brought to a successful conclusion only by the intervention of God. We little know what supernatural forces are unleashed when we pray the prayer of faith.

Ah dearest Lord! I cannot pray,
My fancy is not free;
Unmannerly distractions come,
And force my thoughts from Thee.
My very flesh has restless fits;
My changeful limbs conspire
With all these phantoms of the mind
My inner self to tire.
I cannot pray; yet, Lord! Thou knowst
The pain it is to me
To have my vainly struggling thoughts
Thus torn away from Thee.
Yet Thou art oft most present, Lord!
In weak distracted prayer:

A sinner out of heart with self
Most often finds Thee there.
My Saviour! why should I complain
And why fear aught but sin?
Distractions are but outward things;
Thy peace dwells far within.

—*F. W. Faber*

PRAYER

Blessed Lord, Thy words are faithful and true. It must be because I pray amiss that my experience of answered prayer is not clearer. It must be because I live too little in the Spirit that my prayer is too little in the Spirit, and that the power for the prayer of faith is wanting. Lord, teach me to pray! Lord Jesus, I trust Thee for it; teach me to pray in faith.

—Andrew Murray

QUESTIONS

1. God sometimes answers prayer by giving something other than what was prayed for. Is this a valid proposition?

2. How can we tell whether not getting an answer to our prayers is a delay or a denial?

Thirteen

Moving People through God

KEY TOPICS
Can We Move Individuals through God?
Intercession and Free Will
Intercession and Predestination

"Why couldn't we?"

—Matthew 17:19

It is not irreverent to recognize as a fact that there are perplexing problems involved in the ministry of intercession. All Christian workers, and especially those engaged in pastoral or missionary work, frequently find themselves in situations in which the minds and hearts of individuals must be moved if the objectives the Christians have in view are to be achieved. In other words, we are involved in the complex problems of personality.

We may, for example, be confronted with a crisis that threatens the disintegration of our work. Or we may meet strong opposition in a work we believe is in God's will.

Or we may be unable to secure unanimity in our group on important matters requiring decision. We may even face an impossible situation to which there seems to be no solution that would not cause serious misunderstanding or hurt someone else.

CAN WE MOVE INDIVIDUALS THROUGH GOD?

In circumstances like these, what are we to do? Can we expect to move independent human beings through God by our prayers?

People are difficult objects to move. Prayer for material things is much less complex and demanding than that which involves the intricacies of the human heart. But God has placed in our hands a key with three words that will open this complicated lock: *Ask! Seek! Knock!* (Matthew 7:7–8).

These three words are often treated as though they were synonyms or alternative descriptions of one prayer. But it would seem, instead, that they refer to progressive acts of prayer, each more intense and more demanding than the last. They represent an ascending climax, stages of increasing persistence. In support of that viewpoint, some have seen in the passage the picture of a needy and importunate man who first asks the aid of a friend in some public place. On being rebuffed, he seeks his friend out at his home and renews the plea with increasing urgency. When the door is shut in his face, he refuses to go away, but keeps on knocking and demanding help until he receives it.

This is, of course, a parable of contrast that enforces a primary lesson. God desires us to be earnest to the point of persistency, of refusal to be denied, and He assures that He will grant the answer to such praying: "It *will* be given to you . . . you *will* find . . . the door *will* be opened" (italics added). We are thus encouraged to bring our insoluble problems to Him and are assured of answers.

But it is just here that we come face-to-face with the problem of human freedom. Scripture makes it clear that God has endowed humanity with the godlike quality of self-determination and free will. That this subject is mysterious and open to varying interpretations is admitted, but it is the view of many evangelical Christians that human beings possess the awesome power of saying no to God as well as yes.

INTERCESSION AND FREE WILL

This power poses a very real problem in intercession. Will God violate the free will of one person in order to answer the prayers of another? If by our prayers we can affect the conduct of other people, does that not involve trespassing on their free wills? And yet, if our prayers cannot so influence others, what is the point in praying?

In our search for a solution, we must bear in mind certain factors.

1. *Intercession is a divine ordinance*, and whatever problems we encounter, we believers must render obedience to God. We are exhorted to make "petitions, prayers, intercession and thanksgiving . . . for all people" (1 Timothy 2:1).

2. *In all God's actions, He is consistent with Himself.* He cannot deny or contradict Himself. If He has bound

Himself by a promise to answer the prayer of faith, He will undoubtedly do so but not in a manner that is contrary to His divine nature. He will fulfill all He has undertaken to do but in a way that is consistent with His own nature and attributes. It is axiomatic that no word or action of God will contradict any other word or action of God.

It could be contended that, whereas our supplications do not change God's mind, they often produce such a change in us as to make it right and consistent for God to grant a favorable answer to the supplicant.

God obviously finds no inconsistency or conflict between prayer and the exercise of free will. When He exhorts us to pray for earthly rulers, there is implicit in the command the assurance that our prayers will make a difference, that they can move these powerful individuals and significantly influence the course of national and international events. Otherwise, why pray? Whether we find an intellectually satisfying and final answer to this prayer problem or not, the fact that God has commanded it should be sufficient to satisfy faith, and we are under obligation to obey.

When we have prayed the prayer of faith in accordance with Mark 11:24, we can be assured that we will receive all that God can consistently grant us. We can rest assured that He will exercise His divine influence on those who are the subjects of our prayers to the fullest possible extent, short of encroaching on their free wills, so as to enable them to come to Christ or to otherwise conform to His will. We can be sure that He will choose the best time and employ the best method to make His influence felt.

But what if the prayer is not answered, in spite of the sincerity of our desires and the earnestness of our pleas? Some light is thrown on the perplexity by the fact that our Lord Himself had to face the same problem. He did not see His heart's desire for humanity realized in every case. There were those over whom He had to utter the lament of unrequited love: "Jerusalem, Jerusalem, ... how often I have longed to gather your children together, as a hen gathers her chicks under her wings, and you were not willing" (Luke 13:34). And on another occasion He had to mourn, "You refuse to come to me to have life" (John 5:40).

No accusation about failure in prayer or about lack of true concern for the people being prayed for could be laid at His door, as it can all too often be laid at ours. But in spite of this, sometimes His prayers were frustrated. Yet He refused to exercise His divine power in order to compel people to come to Him. This is what is involved in the solemn responsibility of being human. We can say no to God.

However, this did not discourage Jesus from praying. He recognized the solemn fact, as we must, that in the final analysis the human will can become so debased that it can thwart the loving desires of God's heart. In the face of those circumstances, He did what we must do. He prayed and trustingly left the issue in the hands of His Father.

INTERCESSION AND PREDESTINATION

Another question naturally arises as we face the problems involved in intercession. How can we reconcile intercessory prayer with the doctrine of predestination? The crux of the problem probably lies in our wrong or inadequate under-standing of that doctrine. But the question is sometimes put, "If God has already predetermined all that is going to happen, how can our praying make any real difference? Would not a later arrangement of events involve God in inconsistency or contradiction?"

This is a knotty problem that has exercised the minds of praying people in all ages, and believers have arrived at different conclusions. The most one can hope to do is to offer a suggestion that may at least give a little help. Since God has commanded us to pray, prayer must form part of His overall purpose. Since He has pledged Himself to answer these prayers, is it not reasonable to assume that in His scheme of things He has made full allowance for all the implications of prayer? Could it not be that our prayers form part of His plan and purpose, and indeed may be the very factor that would bring that purpose about? If the foreordination of God is a valid objection to intercession, could it not also be contended that it is a valid objection to every other form of human activity?

In prayer we deal with God directly, and with people only in a secondary sense. The goal of prayer is the ear of God. It is not our prayer that moves people, but the God to whom we pray moves people. Prayer influences people by moving God to influence them. If a scheming Jacob could be entrusted with power with God and with human beings (Genesis 32:28), may we not, despite our failures, be entrusted with a similar ministry?

When Ezra returned to Jerusalem, he faced a situation typical of that experienced so often by Christian workers.

He found his people in a tragically backslidden condition. He could not preach to them. How could he influence them to dissolve forbidden partnerships, to divorce forbidden wives and husbands, and to put right a hundred other irregularities? He could influence God to influence them!

So he gave himself to prayer and the confession of sins to which he had not been party. He pleaded, with fasting, for God's mercy on His people. No placid and pallid praying this! Weeping, he prostrated himself before God. Before long "a large crowd of Israelites—men, women and children—gathered around him. They too wept bitterly" (Ezra 10:1). Intense and prevailing prayer moved people, through God, and achieved its end.

PRAYER

May God the Father and the Eternal High Priest Jesus Christ, build us up in faith and truth and chastity, and grant to us our portion among the saints with all those who believe on our Lord Jesus Christ. We pray for all saints; for kings and rulers; for our persecutors and for enemies of the Cross; and for ourselves we pray that our fruit may abound and we may be made perfect in Christ Jesus our Lord.

—Polycarp

QUESTIONS

1. How can God, in order to answer prayer, interfere with the fixed and unchangeable laws that reign in the universe?

2. How can the foreknowledge of God be an encouragement in prayer?

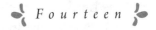

Fourteen

The Pattern Prayer

KEY TOPICS

Distinctive Characteristics
The Prayer Itself

"This, then, is how you should pray."

—Matthew 6:9

The Lord's Prayer was the first specific lesson on prayer that Jesus taught His disciples. They had been listening to their Master while He was praying, and the experience had kindled in their hearts a yearning to know the same intimacy with the Father that He enjoyed. He answered them by giving them a model, or pattern, for prayer that has become the most widely used of all religious formulations.

It has, however, suffered greatly at the hands of its friends. Some neglect it, some recite it thoughtlessly, some postpone its application to the distant future, and only a minority exhaust its full possibilities.

The Lord foresaw the possibility of its misuse, and in the verses immediately preceding the prayer (Matthew 6:5, 7), He warned His disciples of two perils: (1) They were not to pray as the hypocrites did (v. 5), who reserved their praying for public occasions. (2) They were not to pray as the heathen did (v. 7), merely heaping up empty and meaningless phrases.

The failure to heed this counsel has done more to rob this matchless prayer of its deep significance and blessing than anything else. It is reserved by most only for public recitation, and even then it tends to degenerate into the repetition of familiar words with little thought of their meaning.

While not ruling out the validity of reciting the Lord's Prayer in public services, I would question whether or not this was our Lord's main objective in giving it. Indeed, the context is, "go into your room, close the door and pray" (v. 6). It would appear that this prayer is meant primarily, though not necessarily solely, for private use. Do we use it in private prayer?

In this prayer Jesus laid down the principles governing humanity's relationship to God, and these are relevant to believers in every age. It should be noted that He did not say, Pray in these precise words, but, "This, then, is how you should pray" (v. 9). He was giving a pattern, not an inflexible form. The exact words employed may vary greatly in prayers that conform to the pattern given.

DISTINCTIVE CHARACTERISTICS

Several things emerge as we study the pattern prayer in detail (Matthew 6:9–13).

1. *It defines the spirit in which we should pray.* It is to be in (a) an unselfish spirit—not "my" but "our"; (b) a filial spirit—"Father"; (c) a reverent spirit—"hallowed be your name"; (d) a loyal spirit—"your kingdom come"; (e) a submissive spirit—"your will be done"; (f) a dependent spirit—"Give us today our daily bread"; (g) a penitent spirit—"Forgive us our debts"; and (h) a humble spirit—"And lead us not into temptation." The spirit in which we pray is much more important than the words in which our prayers are clothed.

2. *It is brief yet profound.* Only fifty-two words, yet what breadth of application and depth of meaning it holds! It reaches the Greek rhetorical ideal of an ocean of truth in a drop of speech. There is no holy loquacity here, only six pointed petitions. Only God could compress so much meaning into so few words.

3. *It is wonderfully comprehensive.* It contrives to embody in embryo every desire of the praying heart. It combines every divine promise and every human aspiration. It summarizes all we should pray for. Nothing promised to the Christian is outside its scope.

4. *It is of universal application.* It covers all the needs common to humanity. It bears no mark of race or creed. People of every class and color have made it the expression of their hearts. It is the one religious formulary that is easily translatable into all languages.

5. *It reveals the priorities to be observed in prayer.* It is striking that the prayer is halfway through before the needs and desires of the petitioner are mentioned. This is the divine order but not always the human practice. The heavenly is to have priority over the earthly.

6. *God is bound to answer every prayer that conforms to this pattern.* Can my prayer be brought within the scope of this prayer? Then it is certain of answer, for the pattern is divinely given.

THE PRAYER ITSELF

Now let us consider the prayer in some detail.

The invocation. "Our Father in heaven." In the place of prayer, selfishness is excluded. This is a prayer for the family of which God is the Father and we are members. God is the Father only of those who have entered His family by way of the new birth.

"In heaven," someone has quaintly said, is not God's postal address. It indicates not so much His location as His elevation above human beings, His complete separation from human corruption. "Our Father" awakens love in our hearts; "in heaven" engenders awe. And these together constitute worship. The invocation is a blending of intimacy and majesty.

Then follow three petitions concerning God and His glory (vv. 9–10):

A concern for His name. "Hallowed be your name." God's name is His nature, Himself, His personality as revealed in Christ. To hallow anything is to treat it as holy, to hold it in reverence. This petition asks that He Himself will be universally and perpetually held in reverence among us. He is to be given the unique place His name demands. "A Christlike character is the best way of hallowing the name of God."

This petition has missionary overtones. How can His name be hallowed by people who have never heard it? A true hallowing of His name will result in a passion to make that name known.

A concern for His kingdom. "Your kingdom come." In Jewish thought, the kingdom means the reign, the sovereignty of God. Why do not all men and women hallow God's name? Because they belong to a rival kingdom presided over by the prince of this world. They must first be brought into the kingdom before they will reverence the King. This, too, has missionary implications.

Loyal disciples have a passion for the spread of their Lord's sovereignty over the hearts of people here and now, but they also long to see the rejected Christ enthroned and worshiped by all. To this end they will pray.

Actually, the tense of the verb *come* points to a climactic, not gradual, coming of His kingdom. So it is really a prayer for the second advent of Christ, this time as enthroned King.

> O the joy to see Thee reigning,
> Thee my own beloved Lord;
> Every tongue Thy name confessing,
> Worship, honour, glory, blessing,
> Brought to Thee with one accord.
> —*Frances Ridley Havergal*

A concern for His will, and the fulfillment of His purposes on earth. "Your will be done." This logically follows the preceding petition. Loyal believers will cherish a deep desire for the achieving of the purposes of God. They do not regard prayer merely as a means of getting their own will done, but as a means of ensuring that God's will is done in their own lives and in those of others.

"Your will be done" is not to be a cry of defeated resignation or an outlet for despair. The petition is not, "Your will be borne, or suffered," but "Your will be done." Sincerity demands that we be prepared for it to be done first in ourselves. The significance of this petition would be, "Enable us to obey Your revealed will as fully and as joyously as it is done by the angels in heaven."

We must not forget that, in the ultimate, the will of God is a joyous thing. "I delight to do thy will" (Psalm 40:8 KJV). "Shall I not drink the cup the Father has given me?" (John 18:11). These are expressions of exultation, not gloomy resignation. The will of God is something positively good to be embraced.

> Heaven's music chimes the glad days in,
> Hope soars beyond death, pain and sin,
> Faith shouts in triumph, Love must win,
> Thy will be done.
>
> —*Frederick Mann*

Then follow three petitions concerning people and their needs (Matthew 6:11–13). This section covers the essential human needs, whether physical, mental, or spiritual, in the three spheres in which we move. Bread will meet our physical needs in the present. Forgiveness for sins that are past will meet our mental needs, for nothing so disturbs the mind as unpardoned sin. Deliverance from the Tempter's power anticipates our spiritual needs in the future.

Bread is provided by a loving Father. Forgiveness is dispensed by the Son. Deliverance and keeping from the Evil One are the prerogative of the Holy Spirit. Thus the three persons of the Trinity unite to meet all the physical, mental, and spiritual needs of the believer in the past, the present, and the future.

Dependence on God's supply. "Give us today our daily bread." Although we have our own needs, we are to be concerned about our needy brothers and sisters and should ask nothing for ourselves that we do not ask for others. Bread is referred to as the staff of life, a staple necessity. In this context it may well stand for whatever is necessary for the maintenance of daily life—our temporal needs. "Daily" can here be rendered, "for the coming day." If we offer the prayer in the morning, it covers the day already begun. If in the evening, it covers the following day. The meaning is clear. We are to ask for God's provision for the immediate future. We are to live one day at a time, in dependence on His gracious supply. But people do not live by bread alone. In doing the will of His Father, Jesus found satisfying food to eat of which His disciples knew nothing (John 4:32, 34).

Dependence on God's mercy. "Forgive us our debts." The sense of unforgiven sin and guilt, the sense of debtorship, creates turmoil in the mind. There is a hunger of the soul as well as of the body, and it can be appeased only by forgiveness.

"Debts" here is a Jewish metaphor for sin and is so used by Jesus elsewhere. A debt is an obligation incurred; in this instance God has placed upon us an obligation that we have failed to discharge. This obligation embraces sins of omission and of commission. We have robbed both God and other people of their due. We need forgiveness, and for this we are entirely dependent on God.

It may be asked, "But if my sins were all forgiven when I came to the Cross of Christ, why is there need to ask for forgiveness again?" The answer is that we live in a polluted and defiling world. Although our sins have been forgiven fully and we have been pardoned in the judicial sense because we have exercised faith in Christ, we do sin after conversion. For these sins we need forgiveness.

There are two aspects of forgiveness:

1. Judicial forgiveness is granted by God as moral governor of the universe because of the atonement of Christ. As a result of this forgiveness, "everyone who believes is set free from every sin, a justification you were not able to obtain under the law of Moses" (Acts 13:39). God's law now has nothing against us.

2. Paternal forgiveness is bestowed by our Father upon confession of our sins; it is forgiveness within the family. Christ's words to Peter illustrate this aspect of forgiveness. When Jesus wanted to wash Peter's feet, Peter protested: "'Lord, are you going to wash my feet? . . . No, . . . you shall never wash my feet.' Jesus answered, 'Unless I wash you, you have no part with me.' 'Then, Lord,' Simon Peter replied, 'not just my feet but my hands and my head as well!' Jesus answered, 'Those who have had a bath need only to wash their feet; their whole body is clean'" (John 13:6–10).

Here Jesus makes a distinction between the bathing of the whole body and the washing of the feet, between regeneration and the daily cleansing and forgiveness for defilement contracted in this defiling world. Sin always breaks fellowship and requires forgiveness.

Note too that the petition is not, "Forgive us our debts *because* we forgive" others, but "*as* we also have forgiven" others. The channel of paternal forgiveness is blocked as long as we do not forgive others.

Dependence on God's power. "And lead us not into temptation, but deliver us from the evil one" (Matthew 6:13). This is a double-barreled request. Temptation in Scripture is used in two senses. It can mean either trial and testing, or incitement to evil. James assures us that God never incites to evil (James 1:13). So in relation to God, the word carries the first meaning, trial or testing. God subjects His children to testing to eliminate the dross from the gold in their characters and to strengthen and establish them in holiness. The Devil tempts in order to induce them to fall into sin.

This petition, then, is primarily a prayer for protection in time of testing and danger, when we are open to attacks from the Evil One. Secondarily, it is a prayer for deliverance when we are enticed by the Devil to sin. "And lead us not into temptation" voices the human shrinking from testing that holds the possibility of failure and falling into sin. "Deliver us from the evil one" is a cry for deliverance in the hour of temptation to evil.

Taken together, the double petition would mean, "Father, spare me this trial, but if in Your wisdom You see it to be necessary for Your glory and my spiritual development, give me the strength to come through it triumphantly and unscathed in the conflict with the Evil One." It is, however, a vain exercise to pray, "lead us not into temptation," if we voluntarily and unnecessarily place ourselves in situations where we find it easy to sin.

The Doxology. "For yours is the kingdom, and the power, and the glory, forever. Amen." Although this doxology does not appear in the main manuscripts from which the New Testament is translated, it was used by the church from very early times. It appears in the Didache, an early church document of the second century. Although apparently not a part of the prayer as the Lord gave it, it is entirely in keeping with its spirit and affords a fitting climax of adoration to this, the incomparable prayer.

PRAYER

O Thou who art the only begotten Son, teach us to pray, "Our Father." We thank Thee, Lord, for these living, blessed words which Thou hast given us. We thank Thee for the millions who in them have learnt to know and worship the Father, and for what they have been to us. We look to Thee to lead us deeper into their meaning: do it, we pray Thee, for Thy Name's sake.

—Andrew Murray

QUESTIONS

1. How is it possible for a prayer with which we are so familiar to remain fresh?

2. Are our own prayers really following the pattern of prayer the Lord gave? We should check them occasionally according to that criterion.

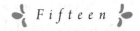

Fifteen

Paul, Man of Prayer

KEY TOPIC

Characteristics of Paul's Prayers

... always keep on praying ...

—Ephesians 6:18

We learn truth best when we see it expressed in a human personality, and this is true also of prayer. In all ages, few, if any, have excelled the apostle Paul in the depth and the effectiveness of their prayer lives. He was at his best in his prayers. In no area of life did he set a more noble and stimulating example. We must be grateful for the self-revelation and insight into prayer with which his letters are studded.

Nowhere does he attempt to explain the possibility or defend the reasonableness of praying. He just takes it for granted and proceeds on the assumption that it is the normal and inevitable function of the regenerate soul and the natural expression of the spiritual life.

He saw prayer as flowing naturally from the filial relationship that exists between God and His children. Because we are His children, He has sent His Spirit into our hearts, as a result of which we cry with great naturalness, "*Abba!* Father!" (Galatians 4:6). This sense of fatherhood provides a rational basis for prayer, for it is perfectly normal for children to have uninhibited communion with their father.

To Paul, the supernatural presented no problems. After his own supernatural conversion, anything became possible. To expect the intervention of God in his own affairs and the affairs of humanity was axiomatic, and he acted consistently with that expectation. He knew no circumstances for which prayer was not appropriate.

In the words of Fleming Stevenson, Paul believed that "prayer is not an arbitrary provision for temporary circumstances, but that it is fixed in the ways of God, and in harmony with the settled relations of the world and the laws of human conduct."[1] Accordingly, it was Paul's conviction that nothing was beyond the reach of prayer except that which was out of the will of God.

Paul's prayers did not just happen. A study of the prayers scattered through his letters will show that they were anything but careless and haphazard. Although they follow no formal pattern, they show clear evidence of careful and reverent thought, and they were doubtless the fruit of much devout meditation as well as the fruit of the Spirit's inspiration. "Study your prayers," said Robert Murray McCheyne. "A great part of my time is spent in getting my heart in tune for prayer."[2]

CHARACTERISTICS OF PAUL'S PRAYERS

Let us note some of the characteristics of Paul's prayers.

1. *They were full of Christ.* It is to this fact that they owe so much of their warmth and stimulating power. An old divine contended that our prayers are so cold and dry because there is so little of Christ in them, a charge that can be laid to all too many prayers, both private and public.

It has been suggested that to stand at Paul's prison door must have been somewhat akin to listening in to our Lord's High Priestly Prayer in the upper room. What depth of adoration, what height of thanksgiving, what breadth of intercession his prayers express! "Sometimes his whole soul flames up to heaven like incense on the altar fire." Periodically Paul bursts out into irrepressible doxology of which Christ is the object.

2. *His prayers were unceasing.* "I have not stopped giving thanks for you, remembering you in my prayers" (Ephesians 1:16). "In all my prayers for all of you, I always pray with joy" (Philippians 1:4). "For this reason, since the day we heard about you, we have not stopped praying for you" (Colossians 1:9). It may be objected that such language is exaggeration. Perhaps the meaning would be clearer if we used *incessant prayers* instead of "have not stopped praying" or "have not ceased praying." An incessant cough is a constantly recurring cough, and this is the idea behind Paul's statements. These Christians were constantly on his heart, and whenever his mind was free, it naturally turned to prayer for them, as a compass needle turns to the magnetic pole.

Dr. Leon Morris is quoted in S. F. Olford's *Heart-Cry for Revival*:

> It is not possible for us to spend all our time with the words of prayer on our lips, but it is possible for us to be all our days in the spirit of prayer, realizing our dependence upon God for all that we have and are, realizing something of His presence with us wherever we may be, and yielding ourselves continually to Him for the doing of His will. Where there is such an inward state, it will find outward expression in verbal prayer, and in this connection we should notice the frequent ejaculatory prayers throughout Paul's letters. Prayer was so natural and so continual with the great Apostle that it found its way inevitably into his correspondence.[3]

3. *His prayers were replete with thanksgiving.* He found much material for thanksgiving in those for whom he prayed. In this he has something important to say to us, for most of us find it much easier to see things with which we can find fault. Typical causes for thanksgiving were the widespread knowledge of the faith of the Roman Christians (Romans 1:8); the enlarged faith and deepening love of the Thessalonians (2 Thessalonians 1:3); the faith, hope, and love of the Colossian believers (Colossians 1:3–5); and God's deliverance of him from "this body that is subject to death" (Romans 7:24–25).

4. *His prayers were unselfish.* Most of them were concerned with other people and their needs, especially the needs of his converts and the young churches. Intercession was his life-

blood. His prayers for his converts not only evidenced his deep pastoral concern, but revealed what he deemed to be their paramount needs. Examples of the qualities and graces he coveted for them were that their love would abound in knowledge (Philippians 1:9–11); that they would be filled with the knowledge of His will (Colossians 1:9–12); that they would prove worthy of their calling (2 Thessalonians 1:11–12); that they would be kept clean from sin (2 Corinthians 13:7); that they would be united in love and encouraged (Colossians 2:2). He carried his converts on his heart.

5. *His prayers were affectionate and sincere.* How many of us could say with Paul, "God can testify how I long for all of you with the affection of Christ Jesus" (Philippians 1:8); or, "I have great sorrow and unceasing anguish in my heart. For I could wish that I myself were cursed and cut off from Christ for the sake of my people, ... the people of Israel" (Romans 9:2–4)?

6. *His prayers were covetous*—in the highest sense He craved prayer for himself. He was in no sense self-sufficient. He regarded prayer as a joint operation: "You help us by your prayers" (2 Corinthians 1:11). The best remuneration he could receive was the prayer interest of those who had been blessed through his ministry. He saw the prayers of his friends as a determining factor in his service. He asked the Ephesians to pray for bold utterance for him (Ephesians 6:18–20), and he asked the Colossians to pray for an open door (Colossians 4:2–4). He also asked for prayer for deliverance (2 Thessalonians 3:1–2; Philemon 22).

7. *His prayers were strenuous.* The words he employed reveal the true nature of his prayers. He referred to his prayer

for the Colossians as being a conflict, a struggle; "I want you to know how hard I am contending for you" (Colossians 2:1). The word here is *agonia*. Elsewhere, it is used of a laborer at daily work (Colossians 1:29); an athlete competing in the arena (1 Corinthians 9:25); a soldier fighting on the battle-field (1 Timothy 6:12). The whole picture is one of intense involvement. He described his prayer as wrestling or struggle in Ephesians 6:12 (see esp. KJV).

Bishop Handley Moule tells the story of "a devoted Sunday school teacher who was the means, under God, of bringing scholar after scholar, with always growing fre-quency, to the feet of Jesus in loving conversion, evidenced by a new life of love and consistency. After her death, her simple diary was found to contain, among other entries, the three following: 'Resolved to pray for each scholar by name.' 'Resolved to wrestle in prayer for each scholar by name.' 'Resolved to wrestle for each by name and to expect an answer.'"[4]

It was thus and without ceasing that Paul prayed.

PRAYER

O God, who through the preaching of the blessed apostle Paul hast caused the light of the Gospel to shine throughout the world, grant, we beseech Thee, that we, having his won-derful conversion in remembrance, may show forth our thankfulness to Thee for the same, by following the holy doctrine he taught, through Jesus Christ our Lord.

—Anonymous

QUESTIONS

1. Make a list of the things Paul desired for those for whom he prayed, and follow him in your own intercessions.

2. What was the relationship of Paul's secret prayer life to his life of public ministry?

Sixteen

Prayer Takes Time

Redeeming the time . . .

—Ephesians 5:16 KJV

A lexander Whyte said,

> I am as certain as I am standing here that the secret
> of much mischief to our souls, and to the souls of
> others, lies in the way that we stint, and starve, and
> scamp our prayers by hurrying over them. Prayer
> worth calling prayer, prayer that God will call true
> prayer and will treat as true prayer takes far more time
> by the clock, than one man in a thousand thinks.[1]

A contemporary of his, Samuel Chadwick, a man of equal
spiritual stature, shared the same conviction:

> To pray as God would have us pray is the greatest
> achievement on earth. Such a life of prayer costs.
> It takes time. Hurried prayers and muttered Litanies

can never produce souls mighty in prayer. Learners give hours regularly every day that they may become proficient in art and mechanism.... All praying saints have spent hours every day in prayer.... In these days there is no time to pray; but without time, and a lot of it, we shall never learn to pray. It ought to be possible to give God one hour out of twenty-four all to Himself.[2]

Who of us has not experienced the perennial problem of insufficient time for prayer? We try to excuse ourselves on the grounds that life is so full we cannot make the time. But of course that is only an excuse and not a valid one. Is it not true that each of us can find time for anything he or she really wants to do? Dr. J. H. Jowett termed the lack-of-time excuse one of the cant phrases of our day. It certainly seems to be on everyone's lips. But let us face it. Is not the lack of urgent desire, rather than the lack of adequate time, at the root of our meager praying?

William Wilberforce complained, "This perpetual hurry of business and company ruins me in soul if not in body. More solitude and earlier hours! ... I have been keeping too late hours, and hence have had but a hurried half hour in a morning to myself."[3]

We should honestly face the fact that we each have as much time as the busiest person in the world. The problem is with the way in which we use it. Among other things, the parable of the pounds, or minas (Luke 19:11–27), teaches that we have each been entrusted with an equal amount of time, but not all use it so as to produce a maximum return.

True, we do not all possess the same capacity, but that fact is recognized in the parable. The reward for the servant with the smaller capacity but equal faithfulness is proportionally the same as that of his more gifted brother. We are not answerable for our capacity, but we are responsible for the strategic use of our time.

If we rate prayer as a high priority in our daily program, we will arrange our day so as to make adequate time for it. The amount of time we allow will be an index of the real importance we attach to it. When our suitcases contain comparatively little, they seem as full as when we carry much, because the less we have, the less meticulously we pack. The individual who says he or she has no time is most likely guilty of careless packing.

What practical steps can be taken to ensure sufficient time for prayer in the daily schedule? The pressure of motive strongly influences the way in which we use our time. To effect such a radical change in our lifestyles as will make more time for prayer will call for strength of purpose and a deep dependence on the Holy Spirit. Not all of us possess inflexible wills, but even these weak wills of ours can be reinforced, for you can be strengthened "with power through his Spirit in your inner being" (Ephesians 3:16).

Are there motives sufficiently compelling to cause us to alter the pattern of our lives, to challenge and break long-indulged habits of laxity in the use of time? Indeed there are.

First, and of greatest importance, is the example of our Master. In this, as in everything else, He is our perfect pattern. He always employed His time strategically, and in selecting

His priorities, He always set aside abundant time for prayer. In His pregnant question, "Are there not twelve hours of daylight?" (John 11:9), lies the implications of the shortness and yet the sufficiency of time. True, there are only twelve hours in the day, but there are fully twelve hours in the day—sufficient time to do all the will of God. There is always enough time to do that. Jesus moved in the restful confidence that there was a divine timing for all the events of His life, and He was constantly exercised to keep to His Father's timetable. We may and should follow in His steps.

When Paul urged the Ephesian Christians to redeem the time by making the most of every opportunity (Ephesians 5:16), he was implying that there is a sense in which time is to be bought. It becomes ours by purchase and exchange. There is a price, and sometimes a high price, to be paid for its highest employment.

Henry Martyn of India was a man singularly successful in the art of redeeming the time, or, "buying up opportunities," as Henry Alford has called it. So urgent did he deem his translation work that he found it impossible to waste an hour. Before his eyes was always the vision of nations waiting for the truth that lay locked up in the Book he was translating. To him, the need of a lost world proved an impelling motive to redeem the hours, and in the brief six years of his meteoric missionary career, he translated the New Testament into three languages.

One practical step that can be taken in order to secure adequate time for prayer is to plug the leaks. We should not think of our day in terms only of hours, but in smaller portions of time, and then we should aim to make constructive use of each of these. Dr. F. B. Meyer, noted preacher and author, packed more into his life than most of his contemporaries. And his secret? It was said of him that, like John Wesley, he divided his life into periods of five minutes and then endeavored to make each period count for God.

The secret of Charles Darwin's prodigious achievements in the realm of science, it is said, lay in the fact that he knew the difference between ten minutes and a quarter of an hour. How many periods of five, ten, or fifteen minutes that could be devoted to prayer do we waste or leave unemployed in the course of a day? Let us determine to make more and better use of these uncommitted but potentially valuable minutes.

An anonymous author likened prayer to the time exposure of the soul to God, in which process the image of God is formed on the soul. "We try, in our piety, to practise instantaneous photography. One minute for prayer will give us a vision of the image of God, and we think that is enough. Our pictures are poor because our negative is weak. We do not give God long enough at a sitting to get a good likeness."[4]

"God's acquaintance is not made hurriedly," wrote E. M. Bounds. "He does not bestow His gifts on the casual or hasty comer and goer. To be much alone with God is the secret of knowing Him and of influence with Him."[5]

We should study our priorities carefully in the apportioning of our time each day. Many hours, while not actually wasted, may be spent on matters of only secondary importance. A fool has been defined as one who has lost the proportion of things. Some of us have developed the unfortunate habit of becoming so engrossed in the secondary that there is little time left for the primary. This is especially true where prayer is concerned, and our Adversary does all in his power to aid and abet.

Check your daily and weekly schedules to see whether or not you are making adequate time for the essentially spiritual exercises of the soul. See whether the best may not be being relegated to a secondary place by that which is good. Weigh up carefully in the light of eternity the respective values of the opportunities and responsibilities that are claiming your attention. Omit altogether or give a very minor place to the things of minor importance. Follow John Wesley's counsel: "Never be unemployed, and never be triflingly employed." What higher employment can there be than wholehearted partnership with the eternal God?

No time to pray!
O, who so fraught with earthly care
As not to give a humble prayer
Some part of day?
No time to pray!
What heart so clean, so pure within,
That needeth not some check from sin.
Needs not to pray?
No time to pray!
'Mid each day's dangers, what retreat
More needful than the mercy seat?
Who need not pray?
No time to pray!
Must care or business' urgent call
So press us as to take it all,
Each passing day?

What thought more drear
Than that our God His face should hide,
And say, through all life's swelling tide,
No time to hear!

—*Anonymous*

PRAYER

Eternal God, who by the life of Thy dear Son hast shown us that there is no minute of our own but we may be doing Thy will, help us to use our time aright, that however we be engaged, in leisure or in play, we may stand before Thee with a pure conscience, acting, speaking, and thinking as in Thy presence, through Jesus Christ our Lord.

—Anonymous

QUESTIONS

1. Can we measure the potency of our prayers by their length or brevity?

2. Does God expect everyone to spend the same amount of time in prayer?

Seventeen

Exercising Spiritual Authority

KEY TOPIC

Power over the Enemy's Power

"I have given you authority."

—Luke 10:19

At a conference of missionaries and Chinese pastors held shortly before the communists gained control of China, one pastor gave a striking address. He said he and his colleagues were more than grateful to those who had brought them the Word of life and the gospel of Christ. But there was one thing more that they should teach their spiritual children. This new thing was how to pray with authority, so that they might know how to take their stand before the throne of God and rebuke the forces of evil, hold steady, and gain the victory.

The need of teaching on this aspect of prayer is no less pressing in Western lands than in the East. Too few Christians progress from mere presentation of petitions to God into the area of the spiritual warfare of which Paul speaks in Ephesians 6:10–18.

The Spirit-controlled Christian, Paul asserts, is involved in spiritual warfare with powerful but intangible forces. In this conflict, only spiritual weapons are effective. But they are available, and "they have divine power to demolish strongholds" (2 Corinthians 10:4). Of these weapons the most potent is that recommended by Paul: "pray[er] in the Spirit on all occasions" (Ephesians 6:18).

Within the ministry of intercession, there may be contrasting spiritual activity. On the one hand, our prayers may be the calm expression of restful faith: "Ask and it will be given to you" (Matthew 7:7). On the other hand, they may take the form of intense spiritual conflict: "I want you to know how hard I am contending for you" (Colossians 2:1). "Our struggle is not against flesh and blood, but against . . . the spiritual forces of evil in the heavenly realms" (Ephesians 6:12). This latter aspect of prayer is known and practiced too little in the life of the church today.

POWER OVER THE ENEMY'S POWER

Our Lord made a startling statement to His seventy eager disciples who were elated from the success of their recent evangelistic thrust. Elsewhere, Jesus had made the claim that all authority, both celestial and terrestrial, had been committed to Him. Here He said to them, "I saw Satan fall like lightning from heaven. *I have given you authority ... to overcome all the power of the enemy*" (Luke 10:18–19, italics added).

The unmistakable inference in this tremendous delegation of spiritual authority to them was that, as they exercised that divine authority, they too would see the overthrow of Satan in the area of their own ministry. Nor had they been disappointed. The radiant evangelists could report, "Lord, even the demons submit to us in your name" (Luke 10:17).

This promise of spiritual authority over the powers of darkness was never withdrawn, but a little later, when the apostles lost vital faith in Christ's assurance, they found themselves impotent when confronted by a demon-possessed boy (Matthew 17:19). It was a failure of their faith, not of the divine promise. The apostles in this case were paralyzed by their own unbelief. But after His resurrection, the Master once again affirmed His delegation of authority to them: "In my name they will drive out demons" (Mark 16:17; compare Luke 10:19).

By His death and resurrection Christ has destroyed (rendered powerless) the Devil (Hebrews 2:14). As members of His body, we may participate in His victory, and not for ourselves alone, but on behalf of believers in the uttermost parts of the world. Distance is irrelevant in this warfare.

In the record of our Lord's conflict with the carping Pharisees, we are provided with a picture of what is involved in praying with authority. The Pharisees had charged Jesus with exorcising demons through the power of the prince of demons. Jesus quickly confronted them with the absurdity of their charge:

Any kingdom divided against itself will be ruined.... If Satan is divided against himself, how can his kingdom stand? . . . But if I drive out demons by the finger of God, then the kingdom of God has come to you.

When a strong man, fully armed, guards his own house, his possessions are safe. But when someone stronger attacks and overpowers him, he takes away the armor in which the man trusted and divides up his plunder (Luke 11:17–18, 20–22).

The strong man is, of course, Satan, whose power over the minds and spirits of human beings is mighty, though limited. The "someone stronger" (Luke 11:22) is none other than the Lamb, through whose blood we can overcome Satan and all his evil hosts (Revelation 12:11).

In the passage quoted above, Christ stated spiritual priorities that are all too often ignored, to the loss of the church. He affirmed that if we are ever to plunder Satan's house and deliver his captives, we have a prior responsibility. We must "first tie . . . up the strong man" (Matthew 12:29). Have we not often tried to plunder his house without first binding him through the prayer of faith, and then have we not wondered why we were turned back in defeat? We have left him unfettered, and he has snatched back souls we have endeavored to rescue from his clutches. Too much of our praying is merely the repeated offering of sincere petitions—and this is of course right—but we fail to do what Jesus said, "First bind the strong man" (KJV).

In the spiritual warfare in which we should all be engaged, a fierce battle is to be waged. Demons are to be exorcised and the powers of darkness restrained, and sometimes the battle is prolonged. It is a striking fact that it was seven years before Carey baptized his first convert in India. It was seven years before Judson won his first disciple in Burma. Morrison toiled seven years before the first Chinese was brought to Christ; Moffat waited seven years to see the first movement of the Spirit in Bechuanaland. Henry Richards worked seven years in the Congo before the first convert was gained.[1]

The complete and final defeat of Satan was consummated on the cross, where Jesus triumphed over him in death. Paul interprets the cosmic significance of that decisive conquest for us: "And having disarmed the powers and authorities, he made a public spectacle of them, triumphing over them by the cross" (Colossians 2:15). The purpose of His incarnation was in order that "by his death he might break the power of him who holds the power of death—that is, the devil" (Hebrews 2:14).

Any power Satan now exercises over us is either because we fail to apprehend and appropriate the completeness of Christ's triumph or because we have conceded territory to the Devil through tolerating sin in our lives. In either case, the remedy is clear.

Let us firmly grasp the revealed fact that Jesus has gained a complete and resounding victory over Satan and has robbed him of his power. We have to turn the potential into the actual through the exercise of faith. As members of His body, united to Him by a living faith, we can participate fully in this victory. For the time being and for some wise purpose, which we may not fully understand, he has been allowed limited liberty. But the execution of the sentence already passed on him will be by the hand of Him to whom all judgment has been committed.

In order to exercise this spiritual authority, we must make sure that we are on praying ground and that the indwelling Holy Spirit is ungrieved. We must accept our place of authority as "seated . . . with him in the heavenly realms" (Ephesians 2:6). It is from this position of authority and power that we can exercise our privilege.

Luke records in Acts 19:13–16 the abortive attempt of some Jewish exorcists, the sons of Sceva, who made use of the name of Jesus in their exorcism of demons. But they were trying to exercise an authority that had never been delegated to them. The formula they adopted in addressing the spirits was, "In the name of the Jesus whom Paul preaches, I command you to come out." But the demon in the possessed man, recognizing the fraud, replied, "'Jesus I know, and Paul I know about, but who are you?' Then the man who had the evil spirit jumped on them and overpowered them all. He gave them such a beating that they ran out of the house naked and bleeding." It is a solemn thing to lay claim to an authority that has not been delegated to you.

It would be challenging to ask ourselves if our names are known in hell or if Satan laughs at our puny attempts to plunder his house. Are our prayers effectual in binding the strong man?

Making use of Christ's authority and participating in His victory, we can be influential in binding the strong man in any situation. Only then shall we be in a position to spoil his goods and deliver his captives.

Blest, when assaulted by the tempter's power,
The Cross my armour, and the Lamb my Tower,
Kneeling I triumph—issuing from the fray
A bleeding conqueror—my life a prey.

—*Adolphe Monod*

PRAYER

Great God, we bless Thee that the battle between Thyself and the powers of darkness has never been uncertain. We praise Thy name that now it is for ever sure to end in victory. Our hearts, amidst the struggles of the present day, would look back to the conflicts of Calvary, and see how our Lord for ever there broke the dragon's head. Oh that Thy people might know that they are contending with a vanquished enemy; that they go forth to fight against one who, with all his subtlety and strength, has already been overthrown by Him who is our Covenant Head, our Leader, our all.

—C. H. Spurgeon

QUESTIONS

1. Does the delegation of spiritual authority to the disciples in our Lord's day (Luke 10:18–19) carry over to our day?

2. Is not the church greatly handicapping its constituents by failing to teach the aspect of prayer as aggressive spiritual warfare?

Eighteen

Power in United Prayer

KEY TOPIC
A Model Prayer Meeting

. . . with one accord.

—Acts 4:24 KJV

N o great spiritual awakening has begun anywhere in the world apart from united prayer—Christians persistently praying for revival."[1] Such is the dictum of J. Edwin Orr, one of the world's authorities on the subject of revival, and it is a lesson for the church of our day.

Both Scripture and experience unite to indicate that there is cumulative power in unified praying. Faith is infectious, and infection spreads where numbers congregate. Unbelief, on the other hand, thrives more readily in isolation. A single stick can kindle a fire only with great difficulty. Was it not at a united prayer meeting that the power of Pentecost was unleashed?

It is a consistent teaching of Scripture that, when a number of Christians unite in prayer for a given person or objective, special spiritual power is brought into operation, for their gathering demonstrates that oneness that God delights to see and acknowledge. Did Jesus not pray, "Holy Father, protect them by the power of your name, the name you gave me, so that they may be one as we are one" (John 17:11)?

A MODEL PRAYER MEETING

We are introduced to a model meeting for united prayer in Acts 4:23–31. This historic gathering illustrates the effect of united prayer and holds valuable lessons for succeeding generations.

So influential had the preaching of the apostles been that the Jewish leaders sensed a dangerous challenge to their authority. But because they feared the reactions of the people who were praising God for what had happened, they refrained from punishing the apostles as they wished to do. Having gone as far as they dared, they commanded Peter and John not to speak or teach in the name of Jesus—a limitation the two men refused to accept. So after threatening Peter and John further, the Jewish leaders released them.

The freed men naturally gravitated to their friends, who were doubtless congregated in the upper room, and reported their conflict with the hierarchy. Sensing the potential seriousness of the situation, the whole group gave themselves to prayer. We may learn a great deal from the content and spirit of their petitions. Note some of the ingredients that made that meeting so effective.

1. *They were one in heart.* "They raised their voices together in prayer to God" (v. 24). Prayer thrives where there is a spirit of love, unity, and fellowship.

2. *They called to mind the majesty and power of the God to whom they were praying* (v. 24). As they considered the activity of God in creation and providence, their faith and confidence in Him were strengthened.

3. *They acknowledged the sovereignty of God* in His power over the nations (vv. 25–28) and confidently expected Him to intervene in their crisis.

4. *They relied on the truthfulness and authority of the Scriptures* (vv. 25–28). They based their pleas on the revealed truth of God.

5. *They pleaded their relationship to Christ* and sought that His glory alone would be advanced through the wonders taking place in His name (vv. 29–30).

6. *They offered specific requests* rather than a general petition (vv. 29–30):

(a) Take note of the threats of the authorities.

(b) Grant Your servants boldness and confidence in preaching the Word. (In view of the very real danger with which they were confronted, they might well have asked that they might be excused from preaching. Instead, they asked for extra grace and power to be able to preach more effectively.)

(c) Extend Your hand to heal.

(d) Give signs and wonders in the name of Your holy Servant, Jesus.

7. *Their prayers were answered by a supernatural demonstration of power.* "The place where they were meeting was shaken" (v. 31). God was pleased, in those early and testing

days for His church, to grant extraordinary signs to authenticate its supernatural origin.

8. *They all received the spiritual equipment for which they prayed.* "And they were all filled with the Holy Spirit and spoke the word of God boldly" (v. 31). A new crisis demanded a fresh filling of the Spirit; this is a timeless principle. They received exactly what they asked and believed for.

9. *They directed this fresh enduing of the Spirit into fresh service of their Master* (vv. 31–35), and their ministry had great power.

10. *The united prayer meeting fostered a deeper spirit of fellowship and sharing.* "No one claimed that any of their possessions was their own, but they shared everything they had" (v. 32).

Powerful prayer meetings such as this are by no means confined to the apostolic era. Dr. Jonathan Goforth was greatly used by God in revival work in China and Korea. Dr. Walter Phillips described one of his meetings:

> At once on entering one was conscious of something unusual. The place was crowded and tense, reverent attention was on every face. The singing was vibrant with new joy and vigour. People knelt for prayer, silent at first, but soon one and another began to pray aloud. The voices gathered volume and soon blended into a great wave of united supplication that swelled and died down again into an undertone of weeping. Now I understood why the floor was so wet—wet with pools of tears.
>
> Then above the sobbing, in strained choking tones, a man began to make confession. Words of mine would fail to describe the awe and terror and pity of these

confessions. It was not so much the enormity of the sins disclosed, or the depths of the iniquity sounded, that shocked one. It was the agony of the penitent, his voice shaken with sobs.

The aftermath of these meetings demonstrated the activity of the Spirit of God in response to the united prayers of His people.

PRAYER

Almighty God, who hast given us grace at this time with one accord to make our common supplications unto Thee, and dost promise that when two or three are gathered together in Thy Name, Thou wilt grant their requests; Fulfil now, O Lord, the desires and petitions of Thy servants, as may be most expedient for them; granting us in this world knowledge of Thy truth, and in the world to come, life everlasting.

—Chrysostom

QUESTIONS

1. What lessons can you learn from the united prayer meeting of Acts 12:1–16?

2. Is united prayer more effective than the prayers of people praying separately? Can you suggest reasons?

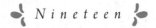

Nineteen

World Rulers Need Prayer

... prayers ... for ... all those in authority ...

—1 Timothy 2:1–2

Prayer for world rulers is enjoined on the praying Christian as a primary responsibility. When counseling his young protégé Timothy, Paul set before him the priorities he should observe:

> I urge, then, first of all [and here it means first in order of importance rather than of time], that petitions, prayers, intercession and thanksgiving be made for all people—for kings and all those in authority, that we may live peaceful and quiet lives in all godliness and holiness. This is good, and pleases God our Savior. (1 Timothy 2:1–3)

Christians have civic and national as well as spiritual responsibilities, and among other ways, we are to discharge these responsibilities in prayer. We should pray for those who hold civic and national or international offices on all levels. Are we discharging our responsibilities in this area? Is it any wonder that the voice of the church is so muted and her influence so minimal in the councils of the world, when she neglects this primary and divinely ordained method of influencing national and world affairs? If prayer cannot influence the course of world events, Paul's exhortation was and is pointless.

Scripture teaches that the church and the Christian owe a duty to the state beyond mere payment of taxes and obedience to laws. It matters not whether rulers are good or bad; we are under obligation to pray for them as they exercise their offices. It is instructive to note that the ruler in Rome when Paul penned this letter to Timothy was the infamous Nero. Rulers may be persecutors or dictators, but Christians are not to stop praying for them.

In general, the early Christians did not evade or ignore their divinely imposed civic and national responsibilities. One of the early Fathers, Tertullian, affords us a glimpse into their practice: "We pray for ourselves, for the state of the world, for the peace of all things, and for the postponement of the end."

Public officials have heavy burdens to bear, and they wield far-reaching influence. Their decisions affect the church, the city, and the nation. We must realize that the hands of wicked people and corrupt officials can be stayed by our prayers.

In the midst of toppling thrones, Daniel maintained his serenity because he knew there was a sovereign God in heaven to whom he could pray. For him, that canceled every adverse factor. He could defy the decree of the oriental despot, for he knew that "the Most High is sovereign over all kingdoms on earth and gives them to anyone he wishes" (Daniel 4:17).

The purpose of such prayer, says Paul, is that leaders may be led aright and that our lives may be lived aright. We are encouraged to pray for times of peace not merely that we might enjoy lives of ease and comfort, but that there should be minimal disturbance so as to facilitate the spread of the gospel. He assures us, too, that, in order that the gospel be not hindered, it is acceptable to ask God to grant us tranquil and quiet lives, free from disturbance from without and perturbation from within.

God fervently desires that all persons shall be saved and come to knowledge of the truth (1 Timothy 2:4). The type of government under which a person lives has an important bearing on bringing this about. China and the former Soviet Union are poignant examples. Although the church could not be stamped out in communist-controlled lands, the opportunity for men and women to hear and accept the gospel is drastically curtailed in such countries.

In offering prayers for all those in authority, we must bear in mind the sobering fact that even earnest prayer cannot avert the righteous judgment of God on individuals or nations when their cup of iniquity is full. But as we pray, we can be confident that as a result of the prayers of the church, God will answer in a way that will be in the best interests of His creatures and will be consistent with His nature and attributes.

PRAYER

Give us new hearts, and renew Thy Holy Spirit within us,
O Lord; that our rulers may faithfully minister justice,
punish sin, defend and maintain the preaching of Thy Word,
and that all ministers may diligently teach Thy dearly
beloved flock purchased by the blood and death of Thine own
and only dear Son our Lord, and that all people may obediently
learn and follow Thy law, to the glory of Thy holy name for
Christ's sake, our only Lord and Saviour.

—James Pilkington

QUESTIONS

1. When we pray for matters of national and international
   importance, do we really expect our prayers to achieve
   something definite?

2. What motives should influence Christians in totalitarian
   lands to pray for rulers who are tyrannical and cruel?

Twenty

Should Christians Fast?

KEY TOPICS

Not a Rite of the Kingdom
A Spontaneous Reaction
An Overmastering Concern

...when you fast...

—Matthew 6:17

Prayer and fasting are linked together both in the Scriptures and in the life-patterns of many saints of God. However, fasting, in the sense in which the New Testament uses the word, has gone out of fashion. "Fasting of the mind" or "fasting of the spirit" is advocated rather than abstinence from food. But to be consistent, might we not just as well talk of giving alms in the spirit? There is little doubt that, when they used the word *fast*, the biblical writers had in mind the partial or complete abstinence from food for a period of time for religious purposes.

There may be some ground for widening the application of the word, however, provided we do not lose sight of its basic significance. For example, the saintly Andrew Bonar contended that fasting is abstaining from all that hinders prayer. Himself an avid reader, he had at times to fast from his overweening love of reading to make time for communion with God. Phillips Brooks regarded fasting as the voluntary disuse of anything innocent in itself, with a view to spiritual culture. Some may find it necessary to fast from some social pleasure for the same reason.

NOT A RITE OF THE KINGDOM

It is noteworthy that, although our Lord fasted at times, as during the temptation in the wilderness (Matthew 4:2), and although He instructed His disciples as to the spirit in which fasting is to be undertaken (Matthew 6:16–18), He refrained from appointing any fast as a rite of His kingdom (Matthew 9:14–17; 11:18–19). While not disapproving of or abolishing the practice of fasting, Jesus lifted it out of the straitjacket of old-covenant legalism into the liberty of the new covenant.

Jesus Himself doubtless observed all the prescribed Jewish fasts, but in all His teaching He spoke of fasting only twice. Indeed, so little an ascetic was He in His lifestyle that they laid the charge against Him—utterly unfounded of being a glutton and drunkard. Nowhere did He make fasting obligatory.

When the disciples of John asked Jesus, "How is it that we and the Pharisees fast often, but your disciples do not fast?"

(Matthew 9:14), His reply was that, since fasting was a sign of mourning, it would be inappropriate to engage in it while He as Messiah and Bridegroom was with them (Matthew 9:14–17). The time would come when He would be removed from them. Then it would not be inconsistent to fast. But it should be noted that He left the question open. (Textual scholars consider comments about fasting in Matthew 17:21 and Mark 9:29, to be corruptions of the text.)

There are only four indisputable references to voluntary fasting in the New Testament. In addition to the two that have been cited, there are two in the book of Acts—13:2 and 14:23. The references in 2 Corinthians 6:5 and 11:27 seem to have involuntary fasting in view.

In a penetrating study of the subject of voluntary fasting, Dr. Henry W. Frost asserts that it is nowhere enjoined on the Christian as a duty.[1] We may or may not fast, as we choose. David Livingstone had very definite views on the subject: "Fastings and vigils without a special object in view are time run to waste. They are made to minister to a sort of self-gratification, instead of being turned to good account."[2]

A SPONTANEOUS REACTION

Fasting is not a legalistic requirement, but it may be done as a spontaneous reaction under special circumstances. Some, like Luther, Whitefield, Edwards, Brainerd, and Martyn, found it a spiritually rewarding practice. Yet there are other godly and prayerful people who have found fasting a hindrance rather than a help. Some are so constituted physically that the lack of a minimum amount of food renders them unable to concentrate in prayer. There is no need for such believers to be in bondage. Let them do what most helps them to pray. Dr. O. Hallesby observes, "Fasting is an outward act which should be carried out only when there is an inner need of it."[3]

The idea that food produces carnality, whereas abstinence from food induces spirituality, is without biblical warrant. It is true that overindulgence in food is not conducive to deep spirituality, but that is another matter. It was Paul's teaching that "the kingdom of God is not a matter of eating and drinking, but of righteousness, peace and joy in the Holy Spirit" (Romans 14:17). He said further, "But food does not bring us near to God; we are no worse if we do not eat, and no better if we do" (1 Corinthians 8:8). Clearly, fasting is a matter in which there is complete liberty.

The two occurrences of voluntary fasting recorded in the book of Acts are when Paul and Barnabas were being set apart for missionary work (13:2–3) and when they appointed elders to the churches that had resulted from their endeavors (14:23).

The teaching of Scripture appears to be not that fasting is a carnal means of attaining a spiritual end but rather that it is the outcome of preoccupation with matters of overriding importance. Dr. Frost points out that in the New Testament, fasting is nowhere the result of premeditation nor is it predetermined or prearranged. Historically, it was usually associated with some strong emotion created by some deep and special spiritual concern.[4]

This would undoubtedly be the case in our Lord's temptation (Matthew 4:2). If the reference to fasting in the King James Version of Acts 10:30–31 is really in the original text, there is little doubt of the deep concern that led Cornelius to beseech God for clearer revelation of His truth. It is also clear that the leaders of the church at Antioch were heavily burdened with their responsibility to spread the gospel to a lost world, since God answered their prayers by thrusting out two of their members who could least be spared to initiate the missionary enterprise. No less a burden would have been on the spirits of Saul and Barnabas when they appointed the elders on whom the whole future of the young churches would depend.

An Overmastering Concern

In the grip of an overmastering concern, these people were led to a prolongation of prayer that precluded partaking of food. To them, praying was of greater importance than eating. The length of the fast was determined not so much by a previous resolution but by the pressure of heart concern. When the burden lifted, the fasting automatically ceased. Its purpose had been achieved.

The conclusion would seem to be that fasting after the New Testament pattern was the spontaneous outcome of (1) the challenge of a special test or temptation; (2) a deep yearning after a closer walk with God; (3) a heavy burden for the spread of the gospel in the regions beyond; (4) spiritual travail for the upbuilding of the church, or (5) the exigencies of a stubborn situation. "These subjects are connected with a large spiritual development," wrote Dr. Frost, "and it will be only the highly spiritual man who will be so occupied with them as to count them more necessary than his meat and drink."[5]

One obvious value of fasting lies in the fact that its discipline helps us keep the body in its place. It is a practical acknowledgment of the supremacy of the spiritual. But in addition to this reflex value, fasting has direct benefits in relation to prayer as well. Many who practice it from right motives and in order to give themselves more unreservedly to prayer testify that during fasting the mind becomes unusually clear and vigorous. A noticeable spiritual quickening and increased power of concentration on the things of the spirit may occur.

Pastor Hsi, a noted Chinese scholar-saint, demonstrated the value of fasting and prayer in his most remarkable ministry. "Constantly and in everything he dealt with God," wrote a fellow traveler.

> In a very real way he dealt with Satan too. His conflict with the Evil One at times was such that he would give himself to days of fasting and prayer. Even when travelling, I have known him to fast for a whole day over some difficult matter that needed clearing up. That was always his resource, fasting and prayer. I have never seen such influence over others. . . . I was profoundly interested in his spirituality and earnestness; his prayers and fastings; the intensity of his purpose—nothing in the world but the one thing.[6]

In the early days of the China Inland Mission, Dr. J. Hudson Taylor and his colleagues had reached the decision to ask God for seventy new missionaries—an almost unprecedented petition in 1881. With a group of fellow missionaries, a day of united prayer and fasting was held. "On the morning of our fast day," wrote one participant, "the Holy Spirit seemed so to fill several of us, that each felt (as we found in private conversation afterwards) that we could not bear any more and live."[7] The subjective blessing that was experienced by those who prayed was not the only result. God answered their prayers and gave the seventy workers.

PRAYER

O Lord, who for our sake didst fast forty days and forty nights, give us grace to use such abstinence that, our flesh being subdued to the spirit, we may ever obey Thy godly motions in righteousness and true holiness, to Thy honour and glory, who livest and reignest with the Father and the Holy Spirit, one God, world without end.

—Anonymous

QUESTIONS

1. Is there spiritual merit in fasting, or is its value only in the discipline involved?

2. Why do you think Jesus did not introduce fasting into the manifesto of His kingdom?

Twenty-One

Praying for Missionaries

KEY TOPICS

Reasons for Dependence on Prayer
For What Should We Pray, Specifically?
Praying for Personal Needs
Praying for Physical Safety
Strategic Praying

"Ask the Lord of the harvest, therefore,
to send out workers into his harvest field."

—Matthew 9:38

"Brothers and sisters, pray for us that the message of the Lord may spread rapidly and be honored, just as it was with you" (2 Thessalonians 3:1). This moving plea from the first and greatest missionary, whose great gifts and spiritual endowment may well have made him less dependent upon intercession than others were, indicates the importance he laid on the prayers of his friends. Note in the following verses the juxtaposition of the hard-pressed missionary's extremity with the part he expected intercession to play in his deliverance.

"We were under great pressure, far beyond our ability to endure, so that we despaired of life itself. . . . [But God] delivered us. . . . On him we have set our hope that he will continue to deliver us, as you help us by your prayers" (2 Corinthians 1:8–11). He believed intercession could be instrumental in delivering missionaries from the plotting of their enemies and opponents. "As for other matters, brothers and sisters, pray for us . . . that we may be delivered from wicked and evil people" (2 Thessalonians 3:1–2). He believed that closed doors could be made to swing open on their hinges as urgent prayer was made to God. "And pray for us, too, that God may open a door for our message" (Colossians 4:3).

As Northcote Deck wrote:

What benison, what benediction would you bestow on isolated missionaries through your prayers? There is nothing more profitable, more priceless that you can ask for us than that, in spite of physical weariness and infirmities and the care of many churches and multiplying converts, we may be enabled to remain on our knees. For there is a praying in detail that has to be done if infant churches are to grow and prosper. And this detailed praying can be done only by those on the field. Only we know the names, the lives, the temptations of the converts. . . . And we? We fall asleep upon our knees! . . . But we earnestly desire "through your prayers and the provision of the Spirit of Jesus Christ," that we might be given enough spiritual energy to make full proof of this vital ministry. But we need your help.[1]

This plea from a veteran missionary is an echo of that of Paul, and it is reechoed from thousands of hearts around the world.

REASONS FOR DEPENDENCE ON PRAYER

Because you prayed—
God touched our weary bodies with His power
And gave us strength for many a trying hour
In which we might have faltered, had not you,
Our intercessors, faithful been and true.

—*Charles B. Bowser*

The question might well be asked: Why are missionaries so dependent on the prayers of friends in the home churches? The following reasons may be advanced:

1. *God has placed the missionary enterprise on a prayer basis.* This is God's method of working to achieve His worldwide purpose. For example, Jesus taught us to "ask the Lord of the harvest . . . to send out workers into his harvest field" (Matthew 9:38). He taught also that success in spiritual work is the outcome of prevailing prayer.

2. *We are members of the body of Christ, and each member depends on the other members.* God does not intend us to operate independently or in isolation.

3. *The very nature of missionary work makes prayer essential.* Our representatives in the front lines are not primarily overcoming cultural prejudices and superstitions but are engaged in hand-to-hand conflict with the prince of this world and his followers. It requires spiritual weapons to overcome an invisible spiritual foe, and prayer is the weapon God has provided (Ephesians 6:12, 18).

It has been pointed out that in this spiritual warfare, the Lord refused to deal with flesh and blood or with the secular powers of His time. His one objective was to deal with the spiritual forces behind the evils around Him. In the woman with a spirit of infirmity, He saw not merely a disease, but satanic bondage. He described her as the woman "whom Satan has kept bound for eighteen long years" (Luke 13:16). To the woman, He said not, "You are *healed,*" but, "You are *set free* from your infirmity" (Luke 13:12, italics added).

Behind every idol there lurks an evil spirit, and this explains the implacable hostility of God to idolatry in every form. The missionary task is to deal with this enemy through intercession based on the victory of Calvary and thus free the captives.

4. *Missionaries are very human in their reactions to testing circumstances* such as loneliness, climatic conditions, unfamiliar cultures, linguistic limitations, absence of stimulating Christian ministry and fellowship, discouragement, separation from home and loved ones, plus the incidental pressures of the work. This factor makes the prayers of friends doubly necessary.

Not all missionary situations impose great strains, but the missionary calling lays one open to many more of these than would be the case in a normal situation at home.

In *Archibald of the Arctic*, Bishop Fleming states that through-out the whole of his missionary career in the Arctic, he was always cold, always hungry, always lonely. What blessing and support prayer can bring to such valiant souls working under such conditions!

5. *Missionaries are usually greatly in the minority and tend to be overwhelmed by the magnitude of the task.* They need the reinforcement of prayer support from the home base.

Joshua and his army were down on the plain, locked in battle with the ruthless Amalekites. On the hill was Moses with his two lieutenants, Aaron and Hur. Moses was engaged in intercession, of which his uplifted rod was the symbol. There was no obvious connection between the two groups. Moses was far removed from the tangible enemies, yet it was he who, through prayer, controlled the swaying tides of battle (Exodus 17:8–13).

The poet Cowper captures the story in four lines:

When Moses stood with arms spread wide,
Success was found on Israel's side.
But when through weariness they failed,
That moment Amalek prevailed.

In the fluctuating battle, the key to victory lay in the hands of the three octogenarians (an encouragement to older believers who feel no longer fit for frontline service). Not arms, but the weaponless hands of prayer controlled the issue. The seeming inactivity of prayer on the hill proved to be a greater test of spiritual stamina than fighting in the valley. It was Moses who tired, not Joshua.

The incident teaches us, too, that there is a cumulative effect in prayer. The focusing of many prayers on one life or on one situation can change defeat into victory.

How should we go about the work of intercession for missions so as to make the maximum contribution? Some suggestions follow for those who desire to become effective intercessors.

1. First and foremost, make a firm resolve and deliberate decision, not without counting the cost, to set aside time for regular intercession. Let only the most urgent happening break into this routine.

2. Ask the Lord to guide you to a special area of focus. Gather all the information you can, and take an intelligent interest in a few missionaries and missionary situations. Endeavor to become literate in missionary matters.

3. Seek a personal link with some missionary for whom you can exercise a special prayer ministry as a prayer companion. Correspond with him or her and follow details of the work in prayer. Experience will enlarge your interests and guide your intercessions.

4. Have a prayer list in which you note the names of missionaries, perhaps praying for different continents on different days of the week.

5. Obtain literature on the places for which you desire to pray so that you have an intelligent grasp of strategic points on which to focus prayer. Learn what you can about the national people, leaders, and churches.

6. Do not become discouraged if results in the work for which you are praying seem meager. Is that not really a reason for praying more earnestly?

7. Leave yourself open to God for Him to lay special prayer burdens on your heart. Such prayers can be mightily effectual.

FOR WHAT SHOULD WE PRAY, SPECIFICALLY?

It has been asserted that there has never been a significant outpouring of the Spirit on the mission field without the previous outpouring of the human spirit to God in prayer. Every new Pentecost has had a preparatory period of burdened supplication.

Our prayers should be strategic and focused, dealing with the great central issues involved in the missionary enterprise as well as with the personal details of individual missionaries and their needs. Too often we are mainly occupied with trifling issues that are at the circumference, while major issues are neglected. A balance should be found. Here are a few strategic subjects:

1. Pray that spiritual revival may come to the national churches and especially to the key leaders.

2. Pray that international affairs may be so overruled that the work of the gospel may not be hindered. Satan is working very powerfully in the political realm, but Paul encourages us to believe that the prayers of God's people can significantly influence the course of world events from the prayer room.

3. Pray that unresponsive individuals and groups may experience deep conviction of sin and respond to the gospel. There are certain places where the Adversary has a stronger

grip on the hearts of the people than others. For example, Pergamum is spoken of as the place "where Satan has his throne" (Revelation 2:13). Only persistent prayer can wear down this opposition.

> Because you prayed—
> God touched our lips with coals of fire,
> Gave Spirit-fulness and did so inspire
> That, when we spoke, sin-blinded souls did see;
> Sin's chains were broken;
> Captives were made free.
>
> —*Charles B. Bowser*

4. Pray that the spiritual tone of missions and missionaries may be kept high and that their policies may be sufficiently flexible to meet rapidly changing conditions.

5. Pray that national leaders may be gripped by the vision of their churches reproducing themselves and reaching out across cultural boundaries into the regions beyond.

6. Pray that the home churches may increasingly rise to their responsibilities in prayer, support, and reinforcement.

7. Pray that God would thrust out new workers to maintain and extend the work.

PRAYING FOR PERSONAL NEEDS

There is, in addition to what we could call strategic praying, the necessity to pray for the personal needs of the workers whom we send out. Elsie Purnell has written an article concerning the special problems facing the missionary mother.[2] If we are to pray for these women with insight and feeling, we should endeavor to think ourselves into their positions and pray accordingly.

According to the article, "Many a missionary mother is frustrated over the conflict in her mind between her duties to her family and to 'the work. . . .' She can find a multitude of Scriptures about her duties as wife and mother, but none specifically about a mother involved in missionary work." What priorities is she to observe? Must one be sacrificed for the other? "Pray that the missionary mothers on your prayer list will be able to resolve this conflict and feel satisfied."

The missionary woman is often facing financial problems. On furlough she will fit into the low-income bracket. She will not have the things her friends and family and neighbors have. Pray that she will learn to adjust to this situation and that her feelings about material things will not drain her emotional strength.

In addition, loneliness can be an almost devastating problem, especially for the single woman. Mrs. Purnell's article has this to say concerning the test a single woman might face: "While rarely discussed publicly, singleness can be the greatest problem facing some women overseas. Some single missionaries are happy and satisfied; others have recurring questions and battles." Pray that they may find a solution to this problem in the more deeply realized presence of Christ with them.

Separation from children—because of educational needs, concern for their safety, or other reasons—is probably the most traumatic of all the testing experiences that may come to missionary parents. If ever they need prayer support, it is when the parting days come. Pray that they will know God's peace and grace abundantly at this time.

If you are aware that missionaries have to face problems among their families at home—problems such as serious illness, bereavement, breakup of marriage, children going astray—uphold them as they carry these added burdens.

PRAYING FOR PHYSICAL SAFETY

Prayer for the physical safety of missionaries is always appropriate and appreciated. There are endless testimonies of remarkable answers to such prayers for safekeeping. Here is one:

> One night at midnight Mrs. Ed Spahr was awakened and burdened for missionary friends Rev. Jerry and Mrs. Rose in Dutch New Guinea [now part of Indonesia] working among stone-age culture people. She was so burdened for him she prayed and next morning wrote a letter telling of it. Later it was learned that he received prayer letters from five prayer partners in five continents saying they prayed for him on that specific occasion.
>
> By adjusting the dateline and time span it was seen that they all prayed at the same time—at that very time Mr. Rose was standing with his arms tied behind his back and a huge "stone-age" savage standing before him with a spear ready to pin him to the ground.
>
> As five prayer partners on five continents prayed, another man in the tribe (there were no Christians in the tribe at the time) spoke to the man and he walked

away. Dr. Spahr asks: "Could God have made him walk away without the prayer partners? God can do anything he wills, but would he? I don't think he would have. I think it was his desire and will to continue the life of Jerry Rose on earth as a witness through his prayer partners."[3]

Paul the intercessor admits us into the secrets of his own special burdens in the prayers he offers for the churches that were the outgrowth of missionary work. They were very like churches in missionary lands today. "I want you to know," he wrote, "how hard I am contending [*agonia*] for you and for those at Laodicea, and for all who have not met me personally" (Colossians 2:1). This brings him alongside us, for, like him, we must often pray for people whom we have never seen.

STRATEGIC PRAYING

It is instructive to notice the things Paul asked for these young churches (Colossians 2:2) so that we can imitate him. He was not concerned for trivialities, but for deep spiritual needs. He asked (1) for *spiritual strengthening*, "that they may be encouraged in heart"; (2) for *spiritual unity*, "that they may be . . . united in love"; (3) for *spiritual certitude*, "that they may have the full riches of complete understanding"; and (4) for *spiritual insight*, "in order that they may know the mystery of God, namely, Christ." This last request is the crowning point of the prayer, for in the full knowledge of Christ, everything else is included.

The letter to the Colossians also introduces us to another mighty intercessor, Epaphras. "I do not know that Epaphras was an eloquent preacher," said Joseph Parker, "but he was mighty in intercession. He threw his arms around his native church and toiled in prayer for them until his brow was bedewed with agony, and his whole face was lighted up with saintly expectation that he might see the descending blessing."

Parker drew this picture from the brief glimpse Paul gives in Colossians 4:12. "Epaphras . . . sends greetings. He is always wrestling [*agonizomenos*] in prayer for you, that you may stand firm in all the will of God, mature and fully assured." Prison walls could not restrain the flight and freedom of the soul of this concerned pastor. Denied personal contact with his flock, he could still exercise on their behalf the most potent of all ministries. His concern for their spiritual advancement found expression in prayer that amounted almost to agony, for that is the word used. This was no mere passive and benevolent well-wishing. He took his praying seriously. The picture behind the word is that of a perspiring wrestler straining every muscle.

What a pale reflection of this are our tepid and languid prayers! How little most of us know of this conflict, this laboring, this travail in prayer that characterized the praying of these two men of God and has been repeated in the lives of many choice souls down the ages!

PRAYER

O God of all the nations of the earth, remember the multitudes of the heathen, who, though created in Thine image, have not known Thee, nor the dying of Thy Son their Saviour Jesus Christ; and grant that by the prayers and labours of Thy holy church they may be delivered from all ignorance and unbelief, and brought to worship Thee; through Him whom Thou hast sent to be the Resurrection and the Life of all men, Thy Son Jesus Christ our Lord.

—Francis Xavier

QUESTIONS

1. See if you can match the prayers of Paul's friends for him with actual answers.

2. Do you have a regular and systematic place for missionary work in your prayers?

Twenty - Two

Prayer and Revival

"If my people . . . will, . . . then I will . . ."

—2 Chronicles 7:14

Oh, that you would burst forth from the skies and come
down! How the mountains would quake in your presence!
The consuming fire of your glory would burn down the
forests and boil the oceans dry. The nations would tremble
before you; then your enemies would learn the reason for
your fame! So it was before when you came down, for you
did awesome things beyond our highest expectations,
and how the mountains quaked!

—Isaiah 64:1–3 TLB

The poet Burns spoke of "rapt Isaiah's wild seraphic fire,"
and the above paragraph is aflame with it. In the voca-
tive plea of this majestic passage, one can sense the fire
burning in Isaiah's heart. In vivid phrase and with moving
eloquence, he pours out his heart to God, pleading for a divine
visitation on his needy nation. It is a poignant, almost desperate prayer, but one laced with ardent faith.

Isaiah gives what Samuel M. Zwemer described as an incomparable definition of prayer: "No one calls on your name or strives *to lay hold of you*" (Isaiah 64:7, italics added). What a vivid picture! "The suppliant stirs himself out of lethargy and sleep to seize hold of God, and he says, 'I will not let you go except You bless me and answer my prayer.'"[1] This is the kind of praying that opens the windows of heaven. There is no tepidity here; intellect, emotion, and will unite to take hold of God.

In chapter 63, verse 15, Isaiah cries, "O Lord, *look down* from heaven and see us" (TLB, italics added). He pleads, "Oh, that you would burst forth from the skies and *come down!*" (Isaiah 64:1 TLB, italics added). He recalls the wonders of Sinai (64:3–4) and asks for a repetition of the supernatural intervention. Then he pours out his heart in confession: "We are all infected and impure with sin. When we put on our prized robes of righteousness we find they are but filthy rags. . . . And our sins, like the wind, sweep us away. Yet no one calls upon your name" (64:6–7 TLB).

The nation had reached the state at which only an invasion from heaven could meet their desperate need, for they faced a dual problem—closed heavens and an absent God. Isaiah had exhausted his own repertoire; he had no prescription for the national malady. Only God could meet the situation.

So Isaiah was very bold (Romans 10:20) and said in effect, "If no one else will take hold of God, I shall. Oh, that You would come down and display Your mighty power!" Have we reached the stage of desperation yet, or have we opted for a continuance of the status quo? Isn't this fire what we need for our powerless churches and sick and decadent society?

Around 1950, there was a powerful movement of the Spirit in the Hebrides. The awakening did not just happen. For some months, a number of men met three nights a week for prayer; they often spent hours. The weeks passed and nothing happened—until one morning at about two o'clock; a young man read Psalm 24:3–5, "Who may ascend the mountain of the LORD? Who may stand in his holy place? The one who has clean hands and a pure heart, who does not trust in an idol or swear by a false god. They will receive blessing from the LORD."

[He] closed the Bible and, looking at his companions on their knees before God, he cried: "Brethren, it is just so much humbug to be waiting thus night after night, month after month, if we ourselves are not right with God. I must ask myself—'Is my heart pure? Are my hands clean?'" And at that moment, . . . something happened. God swept into that prayer group and at that wonderful moment seven Elders discovered what they evidently had not discovered before, that revival must be related to Holiness. . . . They found themselves in the searching power of the presence of God and discovered things about themselves they had never suspected. But the Blood of Calvary heals and cleanses. . . . These men . . . found themselves lifted to the realm of the supernatural. These men knew that Revival had come.[2] [This was the beginning of a movement that went from congregation to congregation and island to island off the coast of Scotland, with far-reaching effects.]

This final lesson in our school of prayer seems an appropriate place to relate several other instances of prevailing prayer that were accompanied by a cleansing of heart and life and resulted in powerful spiritual revival. I present these examples in the hope that faith and aspiration will be kindled in the hearts of readers.

A young married woman (Mary Binnie, who in her later years was known to me and whose granddaughter became my wife) had been converted in the Great Revival of 1859. She was a member of Charlotte Baptist Chapel in Edinburgh. Although this church had a noble history, it had fallen on evil days. Her heart was deeply burdened at the spiritual state of the church, and as she prayed, she received the clear conviction, from the Spirit of God she believed, that it was His purpose to send revival to the moribund Charlotte Chapel. She gave herself to prayer, and expectantly awaited the answer, little dreaming how many years would elapse before the promised revival came or what was to be her part in it.

Then tragedy struck. Her husband was suddenly taken from her side, leaving her with three small children, and twins which were born shortly after his death. As she had few financial resources, her mother who lived in Kelso urged her to live with her. This she was loath to do as she felt she must be there when the revival came to the chapel. At last circumstances compelled her to accept her mother's invitation, and she took her little family to Kelso, but her intercessions for the revival were as urgent as ever.

At that time Kelso could boast no Baptist chapel, so she set herself to pray that someone would be moved to build one. One day, while walking down the main street of the town, she was accosted by a wealthy woman who, in the course of conversation told her that God had laid it on her heart to build a Baptist chapel in Kelso! The startling announcement did not at all surprise this woman of faith who had implicit confidence in the power of God to answer prayer.

When the chapel was built, they called a young man recently graduated from the Glasgow Bible Institute, Joseph W. Kemp. Under his vigorous ministry the church prospered, and in due course he married one of the twin daughters of the godly widow.

But what of the promised revival at Charlotte Chapel? Through the intervening years the importunate widow had not staggered at the promise of God through unbelief, but had persistently pressed her suit at the throne of grace. It takes little imagination to picture her awe when an invitation came to her loved son-in-law to occupy the vacant pulpit of Charlotte Chapel. Was God at last going to answer the prayers of many years? Was He going to send revival, using as His instruments her own daughter and her husband? Then the long test of faith had been abundantly worthwhile.

From the moment of the advent of the energetic young pastor, the tide in the affairs of the church turned decisively. The congregation of thirty-five at the welcome meeting quickly began to increase under the persuasiveness of his passionate preaching.

His lifelong tendency to overwork began to affect Mr. Kemp's health and his officers suggested a holiday, but he spent it visiting the Welsh Revival which was then at its height. There he saw scenes enacted before his eyes that filled him with a longing to see a similar movement of the Spirit in his own church.

On returning to Edinburgh, he shared his burden with some members of his church who were gathered in prayer. From that moment the floodgates of blessing were opened wide. Night after night, week after week the meetings increased in numbers and intensity.

One who was reporting on the movement wrote:

It is impossible to convey any adequate idea of the prayer passion that characterised those meetings. There was little or no preaching, it being no uncommon experience for the pastor to go to the pulpit on the Lord's Day and find the congregation so caught in the spirit of prayer as to render preaching out of the question. For a whole year the church prayed on night by night without a single break.

The people poured out their hearts in importunate prayer. I have yet to witness a movement that has produced more permanent results in the lives of men, women and children. There were irregularities, no doubt; some commotion, yes. There was that which shot itself through all prescribed forms and shattered all conventionality. But such a movement with all its irregularities is to be preferred far above the dull, dreary, monotonous decorum of many churches. Under these influences, crowds thronged the chapel which, only three years before, maintained a sombre vacuum.[3]

Writing of the movement, the pastor said that during the first year he had personally dealt with no fewer than one thousand souls who had been brought to God during the prayer meetings. Conversions took place at every meeting.

At the end of the first year of this sovereign visitation, it seemed as though the tide of spiritual fervour was on the ebb. The pastor made preparation for a course of teaching with a view to consolidating and conserving the wonderful work of the past year. But once again the Spirit of God intervened.

At a late prayer meeting, the fire of God fell. There was nothing, humanly speaking, to account for what happened. Quite suddenly upon one and another came an overwhelming sense of the reality and awfulness of His presence and of eternal things. Life, death and eternity seemed suddenly laid bare. Prayer and weeping began, and gained in intensity every moment. One was overwhelmed before the sudden bursting of the bounds. Could it be real? The midnight hour was reached. The hours had passed like minutes.[4]

The revival fires blazed for a second whole year, during which eight hundred more sought and found the Lord in the chapel. One elder wrote of the prayer meetings,

It has been my privilege to be at some of the wonderful early and late prayer meetings which have been such a marked feature of the revival. He has attended half nights of prayer and whole nights of prayer, some of which will never be forgotten; but in no case has he ever seen anything like what has taken place in the past few weeks.

Here were men and women on their knees, many filled with an intense passionate longing, with strong crying to God; others in bondage yet longing to be free; some melted by love divine, whose eyes with tears o'erflowed. At times the spirit of prayer so increased that it seemed as if all were praying. At another time the soul gave vent in song as it overflowed in joy. The sense of God's nearness and presence was at times overwhelming.[5]

This extended account is given, first, to kindle desire and stimulate prayer that there might be a similar quickening in our own times; second, to show the power and effectiveness of the prayers of one obscure saint whose name never hit the headlines but is held in high honor in heaven.

Not long before China fell to communism, the author was privileged to visit the Chungking Theological Seminary with a colleague, Fred Mitchell, chairman of the English Keswick Convention; we each delivered several messages to the student body. The principal of the seminary, the Reverend Marcus Cheng, and the students had for some time been praying that showers of blessing might fall on their hungry hearts. The principal wrote:

In describing the experience, I would say, "then the fire of the Lord fell." The Holy Spirit was in control, and although the speakers were several, the theme was one, and the messages related to one another in such a way that there was a progression of thought.

The Holy Spirit began to convict of sin. All our consciences were quickened, causing the remembrance of hidden and forgotten sins. The light of the Holy Spirit penetrated the inmost recesses of the heart so that we could not but repent, making confession in public prayer and spontaneous grief and tears. At each meeting, after the close of the message, one after another in rapid succession stood up and prayed for an hour or two. Even then the meeting would have carried on indefinitely had we allowed it to do so.

Classes were suspended for a week that every one might have the opportunity of waiting on God. The Spirit of prayer truly came upon us. Moreover, all general terms and hackneyed expressions were discarded and requests were specific. "Lord, forgive me this sin," (naming it). Some confessed many many sins, one after another. We came to have a genuine hatred of sin.

Not only was confession made to God and man, but as far as possible each made apology and restitution. Apart from monetary restitution there was one who produced articles that did not belong to him, a hat and a torch. One confessed that he had failed to tithe and gave a gold ring. Another said, "I have sinned against so and so who is now dead. How can I apologize now?" Nearly every student felt he had to write letters to family or friends making confession or testifying. Two afternoons were given over to writing such letters.

One wrote thirty. Stationery and stamps became a problem. Just then a letter came from a graduate with a cheque for students' pocket money. It was used for this purpose.

Then followed rededication as we placed ourselves anew at the Lord's disposal.[6]

God had indeed answered their prayers for revival blessing but in a manner they little expected. It was only a short while after this visitation that the communists caused the seminary to be closed and the students scattered. How blessed that before they had to face this ordeal they had put things right with God and other people and had a clear sky above them.

Some years ago a great revival swept over Korea, the fruits of which remain to the present day. This revival had been prayed down. Four missionaries of different denominations had agreed to meet together to pray daily at noon. At the end of one month a brother proposed that "as nothing had happened," the prayer meetings should be discontinued. "Let us each pray at home as we find it convenient," said he. The others, however, protested that they ought rather to spend even more time in prayer each day. So they continued the daily prayer meetings for four months. Then suddenly the blessing began to be poured out.

In *Evangelical Christian* magazine, one of the missionaries declared: "It paid well to have spent several months in prayer; for when God gave the Holy Spirit, He accomplished more in half a day than all the missionaries together could have accomplished in half a year." In less than two months, more than two thousand people were converted. In one church it was announced that a daily prayer meeting would be held every morning at 4:30. The very first day four hundred people arrived long before the stated hour, eager to pray. The number rapidly increased to six hundred. Unbelievers came to see what was happening. They exclaimed in astonishment, "The living God is among you!"

When God plans to send revival blessing, He lays a burden for it on the hearts of those who make themselves available to Him. An aged saint went to his pastor one night and said, "We are about to have a revival." He was asked how he knew so. His answer was, "I went into the stable to take care of my cattle two hours ago, and there the Lord has kept me in prayer until just now. And I feel we are going to be revived." Indeed, revival did commence. Are we similarly available?

PRAYER

O Lord, we pray for our country that God would bless it; and O that we might have a season of revival of pure and undefiled religion in the land. We perceive that Thou canst turn the hearts of the people, as the trees of the wood are moved in the wind. O that there might come a deep searching of heart, great thoughtfulness of the Scriptures, reverence of God and the principles of justice and peace; and may this land make another stride in onward progress, and out of it may there be gathered a people whom Thou hast chosen, who may show forth Thy praise.

—C. H. Spurgeon

QUESTIONS

1. Why do you think there appears to be such a close link between prayer and revival, although revival is a sovereign work of God?

2. Scripture appears to teach that we can see revival whenever we are willing to fulfill the conditions. Does history bear this out?

Twenty-Three

Review

Our school of prayer has concluded, but a life of prayer stretches out ahead. What we have learned in theory we must work out in daily praying, and this demands purpose of heart. God will not pray *instead* of us, but He will intercede in us and thus aid us in our weakness.

Let us now gather the lessons and principles that we have been learning:

1. Faith is an indispensable element of prayer, for "without faith it is impossible to please God" (Hebrews 11:6; compare Matthew 17:20; James 1:6).

2. The petitioner must not be clinging to any sin. "If I had cherished sin in my heart, the Lord would not have listened" (Psalm 66:18; compare Isaiah 59:1–2).

3. To be effective, prayer must be offered in the name of Jesus. Implied in this is the understanding that the petitioner offers only requests that He could endorse. "And I will do whatever you ask in my name" (John 14:13; compare 15:16; 16:23).

4. Our prayers must be in harmony with the will of God. "If we ask anything according to his will, he hears us" (1 John 5:14; compare James 4:2–3).

5. Acceptable prayer is prayer in the Spirit, guided and directed by the Spirit, who dispels spiritual ignorance and

imparts spiritual dynamics. "Pray ... in the Holy Spirit" (Jude 20; compare Romans 8:26–27).

6. A forgiving spirit is essential to prevailing prayer. When a resentful or unforgiving spirit is harbored, the Holy Spirit is grieved. Jesus frequently emphasized this principle. "And when you stand praying, if you hold anything against anyone, forgive them" (Mark 11:25; compare Matthew 6:12–15).

7. Importunity is another element God requires. "Ask and it will be given to you; seek and you will find; knock and the door will be opened to you" (Luke 11:9; compare 18:1–8).

8. To be effective, united prayer must flow from a Spirit-produced oneness of heart and mind. "If two of you on earth agree [symphonize] about anything they ask for, it will be done for them by my Father in heaven" (Matthew 18:19).

9. There is an aggressive and militant side to prayer, which involves the intercessor in soul-travail and conflict if Satan's captives are to be delivered. "For our struggle is not against flesh and blood, but against ... the spiritual forces of evil in the heavenly realms" (Ephesians 6:12; compare Colossians 2:1).

10. Christ has delegated spiritual authority over Satan and his forces to His disciples, and we are encouraged to use this authority humbly in the spiritual warfare. "I have given you authority ... to overcome all the power of the enemy" (Luke 10:19). "They triumphed over him by the blood of the Lamb and by the word of their testimony; they did not love their lives so much as to shrink from death" (Revelation 12:11).

Lord, teach us to pray.

Notes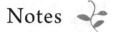

CHAPTER 1
1. Henry W. Frost, *Effective Praying* (Philadelphia: Sunday School Times, 1925), 21.
2. Thomas Goodwin, quoted in E. M. Bounds, *Prayer and Praying Men* (London: Hodder & Stoughton, 1921), 42.

CHAPTER 2
1. A. B. Bruce, cited by J. Gibb, "Thanksgiving," *The Outlook.*

CHAPTER 3
1. A. Jean Courtney, "Prayer and the Prism," *Joyful News*, February 21, 1935, 1.

CHAPTER 5
1. S. D. Gordon, quoted in E. F. Harvey and L. Harvey, *Kneeling We Triumph* (Blackburn, England: M.O.V.E. Press, 1971), 11.

CHAPTER 6
1. C. H. Spurgeon, quoted in E. M. Bounds, *The Possibilities of Prayer* (New York: Revell, 1923), 24.
2. H. S. Curr, "Prayer and the Promises," in *Life of Faith* (London: Marshall, Morgan & Scott, 1941), 2.
3. Report received by the Overseas Missionary Fellowship (O.M.F.).

CHAPTER 7
1. Thomas Goodwin, quoted in D. M. McIntyre, *In His Likeness* (London: Marshall, Morgan & Scott, n.d.), 28.

CHAPTER 8
1. Samuel Chadwick, *The Path of Prayer* (London: Hodder & Stoughton, 1936), 50.
2. Frost, *Effective Praying*, 53–54.
3. Chadwick, *The Path of Prayer*, 52.

CHAPTER 9
1. Samuel M. Zwemer, *Into All the World* (Grand Rapids: Zondervan, 1943), 160.
2. Henry W. Frost, "Praying in the Spirit," *Sunday School Times*, July 13, 1912.
3. Chadwick, *The Path of Prayer*, 56.
4. Andrew Murray, "Praying in the Spirit," *Alliance Weekly*, September 21, 1940, 597.
5. H. C. G. Moule, *The Epistle of Paul the Apostle to the Ephesians* (Cambridge: Cambridge University Press, 1910), 159.
6. K. S. Wuest, *Ephesians and Colossians in the Greek New Testament* (Grand Rapids: Eerdmans, 1953), 145.
7. E. M. Bounds, *Purpose in Prayer* (New York: Revell, 1920), 123.

CHAPTER 10

1. W. E. Biederwolf, *How Can God Answer Prayer?* (New York: Revell, 1910), 199.
2. Mrs. Hudson Taylor, *Behind the Ranges* (London: Lutterworth, 1944), 108, 110, 112–13.
3. Ibid., 114.
4. George Mueller, *The Diary of George Mueller*, ed. A. Rendle Short (Grand Rapids: Zondervan, 1972), 72.

CHAPTER 11

1. Adoniram Judson, quoted in E. M. Bounds, *Purpose in Prayer* (New York: Revell, 1910), 54.
2. W. H. Aitken, *The Divine Ordinance of Prayer* (London: Wells Gardner, 1902), 118.
3. D. M. McIntyre, *The Hidden Life of Prayer*, rev. ed. (Stirling, Scotland: Drummond's Tract Depot, n.d.), 120.

CHAPTER 12

1. H. A. Ironside, *Serving and Waiting*, March 1930, 385.

CHAPTER 15

1. Fleming Stevenson, quoted in Robert E. Speer, *Paul, the All-Round Man* (New York: Revell, 1909), 91.
2. Robert Murray McCheyne, quoted in Speer, *Paul, the All-Round Man*, 97.
3. Leon Morris, quoted in S. F. Olford, *Heart-Cry for Revival* (Westwood, N. J.: Revell, 1962), 83–84.
4. Handley Moule, quoted in Speer, *Paul, the All-Round Man*, 92.

CHAPTER 16

1. Alexander Whyte, quoted in Harvey and Harvey, *Kneeling We Triumph*, 66.
2. Chadwick, *The Path of Prayer*, 20–21.
3. William Wilberforce, quoted in E. M. Bounds, *Power Through Prayer*, 116.
4. Harvey and Harvey, *Kneeling We Triumph*, 60.
5. Bounds, *Power Through Prayer*, 47.

CHAPTER 17

1. A. J. Gordon, *The Holy Spirit and Missions* (New York: Revell, 1893), 139–140.

CHAPTER 18

1. J. Edwin Orr, *Prayer, Its Deeper Dimensions* (London: Marshall, Morgan & Scott, 1963), 21.

CHAPTER 20

1. Henry W. Frost, "What Is Scriptural Fasting?", *Evangelical Christian*, January 1932, 24.
2. David Livingstone, quoted in Harvey and Harvey, *Kneeling We Triumph*, 115.
3. O. Hallesby, *Prayer*, trans. C. J. Carlsen, 12th ed. (Minneapolis: Augsburg, 1935), 121.
4. Frost, *What Is Scriptural Fasting?*, 24.
5. Ibid.
6. Mrs. Hudson Taylor, *Hudson Taylor* (London: China Inland Mission, 1918), 410.
7. Ibid., 367.

CHAPTER 21

1. Northcote Deck, "Praying Also for Us," *Alliance Weekly*, May 23, 1942, 322.

2. Elsie Purnell, "Women Missionaries and How to Pray for Them," *East Asia Millions*, February-March 1976, 157–59.
3. (Auckland, N. Z.) Reported in *Challenge Newspaper*, April 17, 1976.

CHAPTER 22
1. Samuel M. Zwemer, "The Psychology of Prayer," *Biblical Recorder*, August 1, 1922, 235.
2. S. F. Olford, *Heart-Cry for Revival* (Westwood, N. J.: Revell, 1962), 28–29.
3. W. Kemp, *Joseph W. Kemp* (London: Marshall, Morgan & Scott, n.d.), 30.
4. Ibid., 32.
5. Ibid., 30.
6. Marcus Cheng, *Lamp Aflame* (London: China Inland Mission, 1949).

Index of Persons

Enjoy this book? Help us get the word out!

Share a link to the book or
mention it on social media

Write a review on your blog, on a retailer site,
or on our website (dhp.org)

Pick up another copy to share with someone

Recommend this book for your
church, book club, or small group

Follow Discovery House on
social media and join the discussion

Contact us to share your thoughts:

 @discoveryhouse   @DiscoveryHouse

Discovery House
P.O. Box 3566
Grand Rapids, MI 49501 USA

Phone: 1-800-653-8333
Email: books@dhp.org
Web: dhp.org